Engaging Grammar

Engaging Grammar

Practical Advice for Real Classrooms

Amy Benjamin

with

Tom Oliva
Hendrick Hudson High School, Montrose, New York

National Council of Teachers of English
1111 W. Kenyon Road, Urbana, Illinois 61801-1096

Staff Editor: Bonny Graham

Interior Design: Doug Burnett

Cover Design: Pat Mayer

Cover Image: ©iStockphoto.com/TravelPixPro

NCTE Stock Number: 23386

Library of Congress Cataloging-in-Publication Data

Benjamin, Amy, 1951–
      Engaging grammar : practical advice for real classrooms / Amy Benjamin with Tom Oliva.
            p. cm.
      Includes bibliographical references and index.
      ISBN 978-0-8141-2338-6 ((pbk))
   1. English language—Grammar—Study and Teaching (Secondary) I. Oliva, Tom, 1975–   II. Title.
LB1631.B382 2007
428.2071'2—dc22

                                                                2007003361

Contents

Foreword

Martha Kolln

> *Teaching grammar linguistically is like teaching someone to read a map of territory they've lived in all their lives.*
>
> Amy Benjamin

> *Grammar is alive in my classroom—and I'm excited for my students.*
>
> Tom Oliva

> *Why should we teach grammar? I believe we should teach grammar because learning grammar makes you think, and thinking makes you smarter.*
>
> Amy Benjamin

If you're wondering what goes on in Tom's classroom that causes grammar to come alive, that generates his excitement, you can be sure it's something other than underlining subjects with one line and predicates with two. And while an understanding of these two main parts of the sentence is by no means trivial knowledge, the linguistic approach to grammar goes far beyond the labeling and defining that too often characterize traditional school grammar.

Tom's students are learning to think about the language territory they've lived in all their lives. They are exploring their inner grammar expertise, nudging it into conscious awareness. By doing so, they are identifying concepts that enable them to think about and talk about the language of language arts.

Engaging Grammar: Practical Advice for Real Classrooms will guide you in helping your students carry out that same kind of exploration.

For too long, language arts teachers have been led to believe that studying grammar means little more than correcting and avoiding errors, that time spent on grammar in any systematic way is time wasted. The anti-grammar voices in our profession have indeed been loud and persistent and intimidating—and, yes, successful. For several decades, they have been successful in keeping the study of language structure on the fringes of the language arts and in ignoring the insights that linguistic science has to offer.

In the past year or two, however, grammar has been making a comeback of sorts. Given the calls for state standards in language arts and for periodic tests of various kinds, including writing tests, grammar has experienced something of a renaissance. Unfortunately, the loudest voices in the profession continue to reject a curriculum that explores grammar as a legitimate body of knowledge, instead limiting its utility to revision techniques and error avoidance.

But here at last is a voice with a different message, a message that Amy Benjamin brings to the profession with creativity and humor and passion and that Tom Oliva demonstrates with engaging classroom vignettes. In place of "the dusty old grammar that was full of 'Don't do this' and 'Never do that,'" Amy and Tom believe in hands-on grammar, language study that is lively and challenging, language study that exercises higher-level thinking skills—grammar lessons that do indeed make students think, that make them smarter.

The lessons in *Engaging Grammar* illuminate two underlying principles of linguistic grammar that set this book apart from language arts textbooks based on traditional school grammar:

1. *Your students are language experts*. Before they started kindergarten, your students had internalized almost all of the grammar rules they will be using as adults—along with a vocabulary that numbered in the thousands of words. This expertise applies to all children with normal development, no matter what their native language or their home dialect happens to be. The lessons of linguistic grammar capitalize on this inner expertise, bringing it to a conscious level, and applying it to literacy—to the teaching of reading and writing.

2. *The description of linguistic grammar is grounded in English itself, not in Latin*. The familiar eight parts of speech that describe traditional school grammar were adopted as the pattern back in the days when Latin was considered the language of culture—and when the purpose for teaching grammar was to prescribe standards of proper usage. Today's linguistic grammar makes use of the work of the structural linguists, who, some sixty years ago, described and classified the components of English on its own terms. Studying the way speakers actually use the language, they described a wide variety of dialects and varying levels of formality—all of which they recognize as grammatical. The variety we call Standard Written English is, of course, one of those variations. And while some of the terminology is new and the classification of parts of speech is different, the vocabulary of linguistic grammar does include most of the familiar terms of traditional grammar.

Every K–12 teacher of language arts will benefit from this groundbreaking book. For your students in the early grades, Amy's advice begins, "Read aloud, read aloud, read aloud," so that students will hear the rhythm of sentences, hear those subjects and predicates, the valleys and peaks of intonation. She shows you how to use manipulatives, to make learning hands-on and fun. She recognizes and integrates the expertise of many teachers and researchers in her classroom plans. The scope and sequence she suggests will encourage you to work with your colleagues in developing lessons that scaffold and build from level to level and year to year.

In the chapter entitled "Grammar and Standardized Tests," Amy explains the grammatical principles underlying the various test items used in the SAT and other standardized tests. For teachers who are helping their students prepare for those important test days in their lives, this chapter alone is worth the price of the book. The chapter on usage and mechanics is filled with classroom activities and practical advice for helping students use their own inner language resources.

Amy's thirty-plus years of teaching experience shine through in every chapter. And Tom's developing confidence in his ability to make grammar relevant for his students is a pleasure to witness. As Amy notes, Tom's vignettes are "what good lessons look like: real, relevant, relaxed, and alive." That description also applies to Amy's lessons, along with another *R*-word she uses in summing up the importance to teachers of knowing grammar—*rewards*: "You'll reap the rewards of finally being able to speak 'the language of language' to discuss reading, writing, and speaking."

For many teachers, the grammar in these pages will represent a new way of thinking about language. If you are one of those teachers who feel uninformed about the details of grammar, who may perhaps feel unprepared to teach it, you needn't worry about being overwhelmed. In *Engaging Grammar*, you will be encouraged by teachers who understand your position—who have, in fact, been in that position; Amy and Tom will help you recognize your own inner grammar; they will help you help your students understand theirs. You will find that the conscious knowledge of language structure will open many doors of the language arts: literature, composition, vocabulary, spelling, reading, as well as dialect variations and other social aspects of language.

I am delighted to welcome *Engaging Grammar: Practical Advice for Real Classrooms*. Its time has come.

Acknowledgments

This book would not have been possible without the patient and painstaking work of my mentor and friend Martha Kolln. My understanding of linguistic grammar comes primarily from Martha's books, *Understanding English Grammar* and *Rhetorical Grammar: Grammatical Choices, Rhetorical Effects*. Martha has been enormously influential in the composition of this book, particularly Chapter 3, "Elements of Linguistic Grammar." I would also like to thank Joan Berger, whose thoughtful review and commentary helped me transform my ideas from a manuscript into a book. Faye Gage, director of the Connecticut Writing Project, deserves much appreciation for her careful review of the manuscript as well and for showing a keen understanding of what classroom teachers want and need from a book such as this.

To Dr. Zarina Hock, former director of books publications and senior editor for the National Council of Teachers of English, I owe much thanks for her expertise and attention to detail. NCTE editors Kurt Austin and Bonny Graham have been very knowledgeable and helpful in the many stages that went into the creation of this book in its final form.

Finally, I thank my colleague Tom Oliva, whose eagerness to grow as a professional by teaching grammar and keeping a journal about what went on in his head, plan book, and classroom will guide readers of this book to become better teachers.

User's Guide

This book is meant to invigorate the way you teach grammar. I hope to accomplish this by opening your mind to thinking of grammar instruction as closely related to language play. I'd like to see you and your students take risks, wrestle with uncertainties, argue over changing rules, splash around in the fun of language. I'd like to see you blow off the cobwebs of the dusty old grammar that was full of "Don't do this!" and "Never do that!" This book explains how you can teach grammar without any drill at all, without repetitive exercises, even without frowns or grimaces (on your face or the faces of your students). It will help you pass along the technical tools that students need to understand how language works. By doing so, you will empower them.

You should use this book sequentially, moving from part to part as you teach throughout the course of one year. Each of the chapters takes you one level higher in your understanding of linguistic grammar and how to integrate it into the teaching you already do in literature and language. You need not reach for workbooks from which to assign practice exercises. All you will need is the fine literature you already teach and the rich speaking and writing opportunities you already offer. You will be integrating grammar into your existing reading and writing instruction.

The first thing you'll need to do is to realize the extraordinary amount you already know about grammar. You already know this extraordinary amount *not* because you are an English teacher, not even because you speak English, but because you are a human being. As such, you have a remarkable capacity to understand how words are put together to make sense. You already understand how word order affects meaning and how words change their forms to suit the sentences they find themselves in. Right after you give yourself credit for being an expert in grammar, let your students know about *their* expertise: If there's one thing they come to you knowing about, it's grammar. If there's one thing they have fun with and are interested in, it's language.

You may have a background in and experience with traditional grammar. If you don't, that's fine. But if you do, you'll need to understand how linguistic grammar differs from traditional grammar. Briefly, linguistic grammarians study language as a changing, fluid social contract; their categories and definitions are flexible and their designations more refined than those of the traditionalists. Traditional grammarians believe firmly (too firmly) in the eight parts of speech. They concentrate on formal rules and regulations of Standard English. As a result, many people are put off by the very idea of grammar instruction. It has the air of condescension, privilege born of social class, exclusivity, snobbery. On the other hand, linguistic grammarians love language and all of the quirky things it can do. We want to share our love of the varieties of the English language with students *while at the same time teaching them the ways of the Standard dialect.*

Standard English is the dialect that is expected in formal discourse—reading and writing situations calling for the dialect that is associated with education, seriousness, professionalism, and uniformity. When laypeople and educators speak of "learning grammar," it is Standard English they are referring to. Tests that seek to sort individuals into "acceptable" and "unacceptable" bins (tests such as the SAT) do their sorting on the basis of whether the student demonstrates proficiency in Standard English. Our good intentions to teach students to function in Standard English should not attempt to steal away or beat down the student's own home dialect, any more than teaching someone to cook a Chinese dinner would do so at the expense of that person's ability to prepare a delicious (and equally complex) meal that is traditional for another ethnicity. In fact, just as we savor the cuisine of ethnicities other than our own, we must educate our students' linguistic palates to help them broaden their knowledge about the exuberant variety of the English language. Standard English and regional, ethnic dialects are by no means mutually exclusive, any more than a love for candlelit dinners would preclude one's enjoyment of a great backyard barbecue. Everything depends on the social expectations of the occasion.

Part I of this book gives you the background you'll need to understand linguistic grammar and appreciate how students can use their internal grammar knowledge to advantage as they come to understand how their language works. Unfortunately, many people think of grammar in terms of right and wrong, even good and bad, concerned only with avoiding or correcting errors. As a result, both teachers and students often flinch at the idea of grammar instruction. However, as Tom's journal in Chapter 1 makes clear, you needn't be an experienced grammarian to help your students understand their own internal grammar competence.

In Chapter 2, you will learn how to view grammatical information as a body of knowledge that students can use to generate interesting, accurate language, rather than just as a body of knowledge that helps you avoid or correct "mistakes." Chapter 3 gives you a road map to the elements of grammar. You'll need to start transitioning your thinking from "eight parts of speech" to a flexible set of "word classes" that are understood not only in terms of their categories (noun, verb, preposition, etc.) but also in terms of their form (what they are) and function (how they are used). With this information, you will begin to develop a new mental schema for understanding what the English language is made of and how it works. If your experience is with traditional grammar, you will find yourself conceiving of grammar in new ways. If you have no formal training in traditional grammar, you'll need to reread and absorb, layering new information onto known information. That is how the brain learns.

Part II gets you into your classroom, ready to teach your students that they already are experts in grammar and that they can use this expertise to learn even more and to have fun while doing so. We begin with the amazing fact that we understand nonsense language on a grammatical level: If we were to encounter the phrase "niddlesome ditters," we would know that, whatever *ditters* are, we have more then one of them, and that they are being described as *niddlesome*, whatever that is. We can add a tag question to a statement with remarkable ease, considering all of the grammatical information that goes into that feat: When I say, "The guests want more onion soup, *don't they?*" I'm adding a tag question that identifies the subject (guests/they), negates a positive (not), imports a stand-in auxiliary (do), and creates a contraction (don't). When we introduce grammar like this, students feel invited in, rather than kept out, as they often do with traditional instruction. Chapter 4 shows you how to use your students' natural expertise about language to bring unconscious knowledge about grammar to the conscious level.

Chapter 5, "Usage and Mechanics in Formal and Informal English," addresses changes and varieties in the English language and how we can teach students to adapt their styles of speech and writing to an audience that has certain expectations. Linguists call such adaptations "code-switching." We've included NCTE's landmark resolution "On the Students' Right to Their Own Language" and explained how grammar instruction does not have to be antithetical to the tenets of this position statement.

In Chapter 6, we discuss standardized tests and the demands put on students to demonstrate proficiency in Standard Written English. In this culture of the high-stakes test, we owe it to our students and their parents to give them the tools they will need to write the on-demand essay now required by college admissions tests. Standard Written Edited English is expected. The further the students' home dialect is from

Standard English, the more direct instruction is needed. That instruction, however, must not be condescending. If it is, it will not be effective. Rather, we view language choices as "appropriate" or "inappropriate" for the intended audience.

Chapter 7 introduces you to rhetorical grammar, by which we mean the ability to direct the reader's focus by making certain deliberate grammatical choices. Rhetorical grammar refers to the deliberate and informed decisions that writers make about syntax—that is, the writer consciously arranges sentence components to direct the reader's attention and to achieve such effects as focus, orderliness, conciseness, and variations in pace. It goes beyond the basic naming of parts and beyond the correction of surface errors. Rhetorical grammar is the big payoff, where we find out what we can do with what we know.

In Chapter 8, we lay out a scope and sequence for the upper elementary grades through high school.

The glossary at the end of the book is more of a taxonomy, as we've taken the traditional glossary of grammatical terms and organized them into clusters. The clusters facilitate associations between like terms.

If you are a beginner, remember that new information needs to adhere to familiar information. Read one part at a time, along with Tom's journal, and try out the ideas in your classroom.

Lesson Blueprint

Planning for Meaningful Grammar Instruction

Here is a guide to help you design lively, meaningful, brain-compatible lessons that will result in durable learning. The essential elements we use for lesson planning are meaning, engagement, and content. We consider not individual lessons but lesson series, by which we mean a set of at least two lessons.

Lesson Series Planner

I. Meaning: Why?

Consider the abilities and understandings about language that students will gain from the lesson series. A good lesson series delivers meaning that transcends one particular skill, such as subject-verb agreement. If you want to develop a lesson series using subject-verb agreement as *content*, consider how the meaning of that lesson series might also improve the students' ability to think logically, to conform to Standard Written English rules, and to understand the connections within the English language.

> *What abilities and/or understandings will students improve as a result of this lesson series?*
>
> ____Ability to adjust language to a specific audience and purpose
>
> ____Ability to express ideas clearly
>
> ____Ability to conform to Standard Written English rules
>
> ____Ability to think logically
>
> ____Ability to expand a sentence or a paragraph
>
> ____Understanding about language differences and changes
>
> ____Understanding of patterns, connections, relationships within the English language

II. Engagement: How?

Learning about language should be a social activity, not a lonely pursuit. Grammar learning should be lively, challenging, and fun. This is not to say it should be about "games" that offer nothing more than competition to see who "gets the answer" fastest. Nor should the games be only about demonstrating learning that has already taken place. Any games used as vehicles for grammar learning should call for high-level thinking skills: synthesis, creativity, analysis, and, most of all, evaluation of language choices as they apply to a communicative context.

Remember the importance of playfulness in serious language learning. Through a kind of creative tinkering with language, students uncover consistencies (rules) and inconsistencies (idioms). Engage students in word- and sentence play that stretches the boundaries of English grammar so that students can see where these boundaries lie.

How does this lesson engage the students in a way that is compatible with how the brain learns and remembers best?

_____Communication, play, humor

_____Imagination and creativity

_____Dramatics and kinesthetics

_____Metaphor and symbol

_____Visuals and manipulatives

III. Content: What?

What is your lesson series about? What key terms will you have to introduce, reintroduce, or elaborate?

Using this terminology, what grammatical guidelines and rules do you need to teach?

_____Analyzing language; developing meta-language (language about language)

_____Understanding how words are flexible, morphing and reinventing themselves

_____Building, generating, and linking ideas within a sentence

_____Building vocabulary

_____Altering meaning, affecting style by rearranging elements within a sentence

_____Using punctuation effectively

_____Making choices about formal and informal English

_____Clarifying sentence meaning

_____Other

Lesson Template

Activity Invented By:
Materials:
Purpose of Activity:

Strategy and Procedures:
Directions to the Students:
Assessment:

I Essential Understandings

1 Introduction

"I know I should be teaching more grammar, but I just can't make it interesting."

"I became an English teacher because I wanted to teach literature and writing, not grammar."

"The students in my district have never learned grammar. I wouldn't know where to begin."

"All the research shows that teaching grammar doesn't do any good. So why teach it?"

"I'm very nervous about teaching grammar. I never learned it myself."

"The best way to teach grammar is just drill-and-kill. So I do it for a few weeks and get it over with."

"The kids need to be taught the same things again and again. There's no getting grammar instruction to stick."

I hear comments like these all the time from teachers who are my colleagues or who have signed up for my workshops about grammar instruction. All in all, there's a great deal of disquietude, if not disgruntlement, about the overall subject of grammar instruction: Why should we teach grammar? If we teach it, what should we teach? When should we teach what? How can we teach it so that it's interesting, relevant, and empowering?

Why Should We Teach Grammar?

Much controversy exists about whether grammar should be taught at all. In a 1985 position statement, the National Council of Teachers of English used strong language to condemn the teaching of grammar through the use of repetitive, isolated exercises and usage exercises, commonly called "drill": NCTE urged "the discontinuance of testing practices that encourage the teaching of grammar rather than English language arts instruction." I don't disagree that grammar drills are widely considered distasteful to students and teachers alike. I don't favor teaching grammar that way. There's a much more interesting, effective, and engaging way to teach grammar, and that is through authentic language, with an emphasis on the living, changing nature of the English language, which, like all languages, changes and varies over time. The pursuit of knowledge about what language is made of, how it works, and what you can do with it is a pursuit whose value transcends the ability to correct errors. There doesn't have to be a dichotomy between grammar instruction and language arts instruction. The latter can embrace the former.

The ancient Greeks believed this too. That is why they included grammar as one of the seven liberal arts: "The liberal arts denote the seven branches of knowledge that initiate the young into a life of learning" (Joseph 3). To the classicists of the Western world, grammar was one of the three liberal arts called the Trivium: logic, grammar, and rhetoric. The other four, having to do with numbers, were grouped together as the Quadrivium: arithmetic, geometry, music, and astronomy. Together, the seven liberal arts were (and still are) considered the "handmaidens of thought."

Thus, as a "handmaiden of thought," grammar knowledge is valuable because it facilitates the *ability to learn* other knowledge. When we think of grammar as the art of inventing and combining sentences, we understand it in an entirely different way from the way in which grammar is usually received today by both laypeople and most professionals. The classic view of grammar in Western civilization is as a liberal art that opens the mind to the infinite possibilities of word combinations. But this view has faded. Since the 1970s, grammar has been viewed as having a place in the writing process only *after* the sentence has been invented and now needs to be smoothed over, made presentable.

If you come to believe in the value of grammar as a liberal art, you won't worry so much about the immediate utilitarian purpose of your instruction. You will trust that learning about language is valuable for its own sake. If you use sound pedagogy, you will see that your students are interested and involved in grammar lessons, maybe even more so than they are in other kinds of lessons in the English classroom. Grammar lessons, when they are informed by what we know about the learning process, are creative, dynamic, socialized, and highly engaging. And, best of all, they are based on an astonishing amount of prior knowledge. That prior knowledge—the students' internal grammar expertise—makes the study of grammar different from every other subject in the curriculum. This book demonstrates how you can preside over grammar lessons in which students ask interesting questions, many of which will get your own wheels turning. You may find yourself saying, "Hmm . . . I never thought of it that way." You may well see students socializing their learning, explaining things to one another. You will probably observe both creative and critical thinking as students use their existing expertise about grammar in an active process of learning through discovery.

Why should we teach grammar? I believe we should teach grammar because learning grammar makes you think, and thinking makes you smarter.

Why Linguistic Grammar?

Some people find that explanations that come from linguistic grammar are easier to understand than those of traditional grammar. Linguistic grammarians describe the English language in its own terms, rather than in terms of Latin.

Why would traditional notions about English grammar be out of sync with the way English is actually spoken? The answer is rooted in the history of England, its Anglo-Saxon language and culture, and the lowly status of the English language compared to Latin. In the Middle Ages, in order to gain even a modicum of scholarly status, English had to define itself along Latin lines, proving that the plucky English language did indeed "have a grammar." Then, in the late eighteenth century, Lindley Murray wrote the first English grammar book to be used in schools, and that book became the stamp from which all other grammar books were pressed for more than two hundred years. But when the field of modern linguistics was born, led by Noam Chomsky, Leonard Bloomfield, and C. C. Fries, the English language began to be looked at empirically (in terms of how a language is actually organized) rather than prescriptively (how a language "should be" presented). Accordingly, Fries reclassified and reconsidered the Latinate "eight parts of speech" into a more fluid system of "word classes" that must be considered in terms of form and function. This system, still known as "new grammar," is described in Chapter 3.

What Should We Teach?

Many educators believe that we should teach only what students need to know to edit a writing piece they've already composed. They believe that grammar instruction should be doled out in the smallest portions possible, that no extra knowledge about grammar should spill over unused.

Of course, I disagree. First of all, if a student brings you a rough draft in which comma splices abound, how are you going to explain to that student in a conference or a mini-lesson that we need a stronger

mark than a comma to join two independent clauses? What's an independent clause? What's a dependent clause? What's a clause? What's a
phrase? Some real learning must take place, learning that deserves time
and care. We shouldn't relegate grammar instruction to the margins or
reduce it to little tricks and mnemonics. Doing so, we teach grammar
in a piecemeal fashion that never allows our students to develop deep
understandings about how language works as a system and how to
master its rhetorical possibilities.

So I believe in scope and sequence. And I believe that terminology is powerful, that students should understand the terms found in
the glossary of this book, as well as the basic sentence patterns and how
to diagram them with a few modifiers and compound elements. We
should teach the information that is laid out in Chapter 3. We should
teach word classes and how they have a form, which is recognizable by
certain characteristics (e.g., *noun*: "a word that can be made plural and/
or possessive"), as well as a function, or a job to perform in a sentence.
We should teach that word classes fall into form and structure classes,
with noun determiners as members of the latter. And the whole system
will fall into place when we teach sentence patterns. As you will see as
you read this book, new grammar makes better use of students' natural expertise in grammar than traditional grammar does. You'll also see
that it is not that difficult to transition what you already know about
traditional grammar (if you do know anything about it) into new grammar, because, like the students, you also have an innate, unconscious
knowledge of the rules of language.

I'm optimistic about the value of grammar instruction because
I've observed positive results in my own classroom and because my
colleagues and the teachers in my workshops have had positive results
as well.

How Should We Teach Grammar?

When I was a child, my mother had a friend named Sylvia. Sylvia was
gifted at the craft of sewing. She could put together beautiful clothing
of her own design, as well as draperies, decorative pillows, and uphol-
stery. She had both the eye and the hand for it. When we went shopping with Sylvia, she'd examine the details of anything that was put
together with fabric and thread. Then she'd go home and create something based on what she'd seen. She could do this because she looked
at clothing differently than the average consumer does. She had a trained
eye. And when she looked, she had language for all kinds of structures

in the piece. If Sylvia had been a writer, she'd have known her grammar. She'd have noticed that some noun phrases have within them adjectives that are placed out of their expected order, and that such placement sets up an interesting effect. She'd have noticed how participles are used, how all kinds of rhetorical devices operate. And then she'd have tried them herself.

I have had success teaching grammar in this way. I teach my students to become educated observers of text, especially text they are attracted to. I simply invite analysis by saying, "Find a sentence that you like." This way, we don't "stop what we are doing and do grammar." Rather, we "do grammar" as we read literature. The analysis and enjoyment of literature is infused with observations about how language is used; this experience, in turn, informs the writing process. Going from reading to writing is a recursive process in which grammar is the craft to be discovered in the former and practiced in the latter.

Notice, Name, Apply

I first discovered the "notice, name, apply" technique in Katie Wood Ray's *Wondrous Words*. In Chapter 2, "The Craft of Writing," she talks about how she teaches students to develop the insight of noticing syntactical patterns in text. Just as the artist's trained eye sees the use of geometrical shapes in a painting, the writer's eye can be trained to notice writerly shapes. Once patterns emerge for us, we name them. Then we apply them. The procedure of notice, name, and apply is recursive. The reader picks up ideas from literature, tosses them into a mental shopping bag, and then goes home and uses them in her own writing.

Ray speaks of the relationship between pattern-finding in text and how knowing grammatical terminology can help writers harvest what they find. "Once you begin to study the craft of writing you will find that the more you know, the more you see. . . . Being able to connect various crafting techniques that you see to other texts you know is one of the most significant understandings about learning to write from writers" (37). About knowing grammatical names, Ray says: "Most of us were taught about language from the outside in, off a chalkboard instead of from beautiful texts, and unless we've been teaching it for years, we don't remember much about grammatical terms because we just haven't used them enough. . . . And if you are going to reverse tradition and help your students learn about language as insiders, then they need to learn this insider's language from you, naming things for them whenever it makes sense in your reading like writers" (44).

Here's how knowledge of noun phrases can work with the "notice, name, apply" sequence. We'll take a paragraph from *Charlotte's Web* by E. B. White:

> Templeton moved indoors when winter came. His ratty home under the pig trough was too chilly, so he fixed himself a cozy nest in the barn behind the grain bins. He lined it with bits of dirty newspapers and rags, and whenever he found a trinket or a keepsake he carried it home and stored it there. He continued to visit Wilbur three times a day, exactly at mealtime, and Wilbur kept the promise he had made. Wilbur let the rat eat first. Then, when Templeton couldn't hold another mouthful, Wilbur would eat. As a result of overeating, Templeton grew bigger and fatter than any rat you ever saw. He was gigantic. He was as big as a young woodchuck. (174)

I'd like to explain two concepts of linguistic grammar here: noun phrase and nominal. A *noun phrase* is a noun plus its modifiers. We call the noun that is being modified the headword of the noun phrase. A noun phrase is usually announced by what we call a noun determiner, which is often an article—*a, an, the*—or a possessive pronoun (*my big dog*). A noun phrase can even include prepositional phrases, appositives, and verbal structures and other modifiers coming before or after the headword (*a big dog, a dog with floppy ears and eyes that sparkle*) A *nominal* is *any* structure (single word, phrase, or clause) that functions the way the noun phrase functions. A nominal can be replaced by a pronoun: *it* for singular; *they/them* for plural. All of these terms are explained further in Chapter 3.

Accordingly, one of the ways to teach students to identify nominals is by substituting pronouns. You will see that the process of substituting noun phrases with pronouns allows you to identify the parameters of the subject of the sentence. Below, I've boldfaced the noun phrases in the *Charlotte's Web* extract and followed each by the pronoun that could replace it.

> **Templeton** (he) moved indoors when **winter** (it) came. **His ratty home under the pig trough** (It) was too chilly, so he fixed himself **a cozy nest** (it) in **the barn** (it) behind **the grain bins** (them). He lined it with **bits of dirty newspapers and rags** (them), and whenever he found **a trinket or a keepsake** (it) he carried it home and stored it there. He continued to visit **Wilbur** (him) three times a day, exactly at **mealtime** (it) and **Wilbur** (he) kept **the promise he had made** (it). **Wilbur** (He) let **the rat** (it) eat first. Then, when **Templeton** (he) couldn't hold **another mouthful** (it), **Wilbur** (he) would eat. As **a result of overeating** (it), **Templeton** (he) grew

bigger and fatter than **any rat you ever saw** (it). He was gigantic.
He was as big as **a young woodchuck** (it).

I have seen how, when students know about grammar, many
other doors of English language arts open up to them in literature, composition, language history, vocabulary, even spelling. A person who has
been taught grammar in an active and enlightened manner is in a position to learn more about academic and social language, to craft and read
complicated sentences simply because that person can speak objectively
about language. As members of the community of speakers of English,
we are entitled to be players in the game of language, a game that allows us to adapt, adjust, even invent. So my purpose in this book is to
show you how to infuse grammar instruction into all facets of your
English classroom to strengthen your students' entire experience as
learners, throughout their days in school, throughout their lives.

Although "notice, name, apply" practice is useful, it needs to be
centered in an overall framework of how the English language works.
Without that framework, we're back to teaching grammar in a piecemeal fashion, so I refer you again to Chapter 3.

A Teacher's Journal

Meet Tom Oliva. Tom was my younger colleague at Hendrick Hudson
High School in Montrose, New York. Tom has a well-deserved reputation as a great English teacher, though he's relatively new to the school.
His students love coming to class because Tom's creative ideas enliven
the process of learning English. Yet, like so many fine English teachers,
Tom had never really integrated grammar into English instruction except as an add-on last step on the to-do list in the writing process. And
even then, grammar's only role was to correct pesky errors. I've encouraged Tom to take the risk of letting me help him teach grammar.

Here's how Tom felt about jumping into grammar instruction
before he really felt that he knew what he was doing. (Note that throughout this book Tom's journal entries are signaled typographically by a
different font.)

It's no secret: Grammar exists. So why did I, an avid reader and writer, so
blatantly avoid it? In order to become a better teacher and a better student, I had to acknowledge that grammar is important but that I feel uncomfortable with it, and that without my help, generations of young readers will continue to struggle and feel as I do. Honestly, I feel funny even
writing this. What will happen to me when the world finds out I never learned
grammar?

Simply mention the word and my spine goes icy. Maybe it's my liberal nature; I don't like things too rigid. Maybe it's an acknowledgment that after years of sidestepping grammar's mazes and manuals with a crafty, personalized bag of tricks, I might have to admit I still have a lot to learn.

My reputation is on the line here. I'm a good teacher. I prepare my students with necessary skills while helping them realize how a better understanding of the English language coincides with a more fulfilling life. With some serious nudging, six years of teaching experience, and an open mind, I decide that it *is* time to face my grammar demons. Here goes.

Grammar, Day 1

I select "Communication Breakdown" by Led Zeppelin to wake up my first-period ninth graders. As its loud, staccato rhythms bounce off the walls and into their tired ears, I'm at the board writing: *Margaret slept*. They look baffled, not an unfamiliar sight, by the coupling of the blaring tune and the stark simplicity of the black phrase on the whiteboard.

They dutifully copy the sentence in a state of rote bliss; if only the entire lesson were notes on the board. . . . But, although this will keep them numb, it isn't how students really learn. I ask for two volunteers. "Who wants to be Margaret?" Jordan, an eager young man decked out in athletic apparel, raises his hand. He hops up and stands, awkwardly bouncing from one foot to the other, underneath the word *Margaret*. After some encouragement, Brittany, bright but subdued, becomes our *slept*. Still lethargic despite my attempt with the song, she puts two desks together and exclaims, "Well, if I'm sleeping, I can lie down, right?" We are on our way.

Tom is on his way to getting grammar instruction into his classroom. He's started by establishing that his students are already experts in grammar: They are human. And they are humans who speak English. So they know that the two-word sentence is about something or someone who does, is, or has something. Tom has animated the process of learning grammar by having students act out its drama, a drama that is set in motion when subject meets verb.

I tell the students that *Margaret slept* is a simple sentence and that by looking closely at its components we will build a foundation for feeling comfortable and confident with more complex sentences. My enthusiasm is muted by uncertainty. I know that the lesson must seem trivial to them and that it has potential for myriad uncertainties. Somewhere in south Jersey, my mother, a lifelong elementary school teacher, is guilt-tripping me for my disregard of her efforts in that setting.

I ask the rest of the class to divide the sentence into parts. They decide that *Margaret* is the subject, to which I add on the board, "what we are talking about," and that *slept* is the verb, or predicate, to which I add on the board, "what the subject is doing." They are thrilled with their amazing talent.

Breaking out a bag of candy, I ask the students to come up with as many ways as possible to change the subject without changing the basic meaning of the sentence. As a reward, and to help maintain their first-period performance, I offer a piece of candy to the student who produces the best result. Walking the room, I notice Jessica has written *She* and is now avoiding eye contact with the entire room while gnawing at the end of her pen. Maybe we're not rehashing so much after all. Maybe she really can use a refresher course. Penny has a lengthy, meticulously organized list including *she, her, I, the woman,* and *the girl.* Penny gets the candy, but so does everyone else. We are ready for the next step.

Tom didn't make the common mistake of announcing something like: "We're going to start a grammar unit today. Now, I know you've had this before, but you guys are still making the same mistakes again and again, and we're going to learn this once and for all." Or: "OK, guys, we're going to start doing some grammar. I know, I know. I don't like this any more than you do, but the sooner we get through it, the sooner we can get back to the good stuff." Tom said nothing about learning grammar. He just started right in by inviting the students to play.

The students are upbeat about the activity, seemingly oblivious to its simplicity thanks to the active, independent, and open-ended nature of the tasks. I too am excited by their energy and focus. I explain that every sentence is, in fact, some version of this sentence: Every sentence connects something we are talking about (subject) to what we are saying about it (predicate). In other words, every word falls into the subject camp or the predicate camp.

We review their lists of possible *Margaret* substitutes, writing them over our "subject" model (Jordan), discussing as we go. To add to the conversation, which remains informal and unintimidating, I tell them that by saying "It is true that . . ." in front of a sentence we can always determine whether any group of words *is* a sentence. This leads to an even livelier atmosphere as students offer fragments to test the theory. With things going so well, I know I'm headed for a fall, and soon enough I'm dropping like a rock. Esther realizes that sentences that begin with words like *but* don't "sound right." I have no immediate answer, knowing only that these words are called conjunctions, and graciously accept defeat the only way I have ever known—through honesty. I tell the students that I will consult Mrs. Benjamin for clarification. Surprisingly, they don't challenge my knowledge base, and for a moment we are intellectual equals, exploring learning together.

Get used to being unable to answer students' questions. It's what happens when you are teaching grammar in an interesting way. It means that students are curious, and it means you get the chance to model the thinking and learning process.

A little rattled by the awkwardness I wanted so badly to avoid, I press on to the final activity of the lesson. I ask the students to team up with a partner. Using an excerpt from their own writing folders, students are to choose any sentence and break it into its basic two parts. Invigorated and confident, they get to work. After five minutes, we reconvene to discuss their findings. Each pair writes one sentence on the board and, using a different-colored marker, identifies the division. With the period winding down, we experiment with the two parts using the "It is true that . . ." model. It is clear to them that the subject or predicate alone doesn't make a sentence.

So my first foray into teaching grammar is a success. I can't help but wonder if I experienced such lessons in my own school days. How did they seep into my writing and reading skills without leaving any trace in my memory? Nonetheless, I know that my students are on their way up the grammar ladder that has always eluded me. The simplicity of the activity is overshadowed by the students' confidence and understanding of the concepts, coupled with the firm foundation established.

Establishing that a sentence has two parts, a subject and a predicate, may not seem like much, nor is it likely to be a new idea. What's different and important here is that Tom has begun to make grammar instruction interesting and accessible. He's turned it into active, animated learning, building his own confidence along the way.

Grammar, Day 2

I have about twenty minutes to work with today. The second half of the period will have us working on an essay and some questions about bias-free language. But for today's "sentence-breaking" activity, we have LEGOs!

So again I write *Margaret slept* on the board. I keep one eye on the students' faces, looking for pained expressions. To my surprise, there are none. If anything, students appear pleased to see something comfortable and familiar. I know this is a good sign, but my real excitement is about my soon-to-be-revealed bag of tricks. Leaning down behind my desk, I bring out a colorful bag of LEGOs, on loan from Amy. Immediately, the boys become voluble, barely able to stay in their seats. My own gender bias is soon exposed—the girls act the same way!

I give each student one purple and one yellow LEGO piece. I explain that purple represents the subject and yellow represents the predicate. This point is further illustrated when I hold up the two colors and alternately repeat "Margaret" (holding purple), "subject" (holding purple), "slept" (holding yellow), "predicate" (holding yellow). There is a buzz in the room. Emily and Alice fiddle with the familiar shapes; Tim is crashing them together, imitating his younger self. Everyone is curious about the lesson.

Because grammar is all about components, color-coded manipulatives that fit together make the perfect abstract representational system. Even though Tom's grammar instruction is only two days old, students have forgotten all about exercise books, prescriptions, and things that are "wrong" to say.

I ask the students to write a quick story that includes four to six two-word sentences. I explain that they must use actions verbs for the activity to work. I'm worried that this will spark an uncomfortable conversation about concepts that I can't articulate, but the students are already absorbed in thought and discussions with their peers. On the board, I write, *He shoots. He scores. He celebrates.* My example is clear enough; they scribble in their notebooks, eager to impress with creativity. I give students about five minutes to perfect their stories, continually reminding them to use the LEGOs as a visual.

After five minutes, I don't need to ask for volunteers. They're ready to go. It's a teacher's dream—a sea of hands. Noah, always the gentleman, offers, *He eats. He gags. He pukes. He sleeps.* His peers agree, laughing, that this is a fine example. Most students are right on track, but a few realize that their verbs don't seem to work. Is my blood pressure rising? Will my inadequacies surface? How will I respond when I don't know the answer?

Students are learning an essential concept in grammar: patterns. They will be in position later to learn that a verb that can fulfill the predicate slot in a two-slot pattern is an intransitive verb. Right now, they think they are just having fun, but they're imprinting in their minds a visual that represents a pattern.

Kirby and Nicole, decked out in matching volleyball attire, have been working together. Their story reads: *She smells. She bathes. She is clean.* Wait a second! We all realize that something is wrong. Besides violating my two-word sentence rule, their story exposes some interesting issues. We review linking verbs and sense verbs, openly discussing how these verbs differ from action verbs. I don't have all the answers, but we reach logical conclusions and the students let me stay.

This is a typical example of how teachers have to trust that the students are going to trust them when the pattern goes out of control a bit. Patterns are strong. Whether or not we can name things, we can recognize when something is outside the pattern. Right now, Tom's students don't know how to name patterns and slots. But it's interesting that they recognize that the *be* pattern sentence is not the same as the Subject–Intransitive Verb pattern.

Clearing this up is a bit of a battle, but I'm able to regain focus through another related activity: sentence branching. Of course, my lesson on bias-free language is shot, but I'm running with a teachable moment and that is always a good idea.

Time is getting short. I have about ten minutes left in the period, and so I model the final piece of the lesson for the class. I write three sentences on the board:

1. After a night of cramming for a chemistry exam, Margaret slept.
2. Margaret slept, dreaming of her long-lost love.
3. Margaret, the campaign organizer who worked so tirelessly, slept.

I ask students to talk with a partner about each sentence, noting how they are different. Then we review their findings. Surprisingly, students realize that we have simply moved the subject and verb to different locations in the sentence. With time running short, I explain the three ways in which these sentences branch: The first, with the delayed subject, is called left-branching. The second, with its subject-verb up front, is called right-branching. And the third, with its separation between subject and verb, is called mid-branching.

We hold up purple and yellow LEGOs and repeat each sentence, moving the pieces through the air. I also add that a subject and a verb should never be separated by a (single) comma.

For homework, I ask the students to rewrite their stories using sentences that represent the three different ways sentences can branch. They leave, reluctantly relinquishing their LEGOs. I'm feeling pretty good about this lesson, knowing that, if nothing else, students have a new, conscious tool to use in their writing to create varied sentences.

Right here is where the lesson takes the leap into rhetorical grammar instruction. The students, conscious of the two-part nature of the simplest of all possible sentences, are able to manipulate positioning of the subject-verb core in three different ways. Without strong consciousness of this basic grammatical concept, such comprehension of syntax would not have been possible.

Not bad for a beginner, is it? Tom began in the simplest way possible, with the two-word sentence. Using its grammatical structure as a foundation, and relying on his students' unconscious knowledge about sentences, he built up to the sophisticated concept of three ways for sentences to branch based on subject-verb placement and modifiers.

Tom's lesson has implications for reading comprehension as well: The reader has to link subject and verb in order to make sense of the sentence. As readers, we usually do this unconsciously. But there are times, such as when reading long, intricate text, when we need to call forth our ability to get the core of the sentence—its subject and verb— to step forward. Readers who can use this bit of grammatical information consciously have one more strategy to assist them with reading complex text.

Tom, a novice at teaching grammar but an exemplary teacher of English, is on his way to learning what he was never taught about grammar. He's decided to teach grammar despite the gaps in his own knowledge. This is a risk, but I want Tom to understand that many teachers who "learned grammar" as students "learned" it in such a stiff and sterile manner that they are not necessarily in a better position than he is to teach grammar in a way that makes it come alive. Tom has begun to teach grammar despite his discomfort with his own knowledge of it, but at least he doesn't have to *unlearn* the model of traditional pedagogy.

Grammar, Day 3

"Today, we're going to look at the sentence closely, focusing on the subject and predicate." The approach is a little repetitive, but I think the students will like the additional knowledge, especially when they get to test it out. I begin with some notes. On the board, I write: *A subject, together with a predicate, is called a CLAUSE. If that CLAUSE can stand alone as a sentence, we call it an INDEPENDENT CLAUSE.* Next I write: *Part of a clause is called a PHRASE. A PHRASE does not have both a subject and predicate.* The students already look bored, and I realize that notes and grammar are not the best combination. Jordan and Mark are tapping their pens in some secret rhythm; Alison and Brittany are whispering about something. You can't blame them; it's first period and I'm giving notes on grammar. They need real text!

Time for quick thinking. I throw on a song and run over to my bookshelf. "Hey, Jordan, do you know this clause and phrase stuff?" I ask as I'm thumbing through a copy of *The Hobbit*. "Yea, I got it, Mr. O."

"Alison, you got it too?"

"Yep. Are we having a test?" With this, I'm sure they need examples.

Before they know it, I've got a sentence on the board. It reads, *Thorin had been caught much faster than they had.* It is a little sentence but sure to test their understanding. *The Hobbit* proved a good call. Ashleigh, who had been rather quiet thus far, shouts, "I love that book!"

I ask students to identify and label each clause and phrase of the sentence. They begin to whisper nervously. I repeat: "That was *independently.*" They settle in and begin to copy the sentence into their notebooks. Mark, the first to finish, shoots his hand up: "*Thorin had been caught* is a clause because it has a subject and a verb, and the rest is a phrase because it doesn't." Most of the class has the same answer, which of course is fine. But I realize that the simple little sentence has some secrets that these students don't quite grasp. I want them to see that *. . . they had* must be some kind of clause because it has a subject and a verb. So I ask them to identify the nouns and verbs in the sentence. "Pronouns are nouns, right?" asks Brittany.

"Yes. . . . Well, yes and no. Pronouns are words that stand in for nominals." They look a little bewildered. I regroup, realizing that the period is winding down and I haven't even skimmed the surface of my lesson. Grammar lessons have a way of getting away from you.

Yes, they do, but that's when you know you're "doing it right." What's going on in Tom's class is a wonderful discovery process, leading students to ask interesting questions, questions that stump you. Are pronouns nouns? Well, they do function as nouns do, but traditional grammarians don't have it right when they define a pronoun as a word that "takes the place of a noun." In fact, a pronoun takes the place of—stands in for, if you will—not necessarily a noun but a *nominal*. Big difference. A *nominal* is any structure that functions as a noun phrase does, such as a subject or direct object or object of a preposition: *Flying kites* is *fun* (a gerund as subject); *I wonder where Joe lives* (a noun clause as direct object). Although traditional grammarians don't use the term *noun phrase* or *nominal*, these are very important terms to start using because nouns tend to appear with other words (modifiers and determiners) that stick, grammatically speaking, together. I think of a noun phrase as a noun with its entourage. The *noun plus entourage* is usually announced by a determiner (articles—*a, an, the*; possessive nouns and pronouns—*Tom's, his, her, its*, etc.; demonstrative pronouns—*this, that, these, those*; indefinite pronouns—*some, every*, all numbers, etc.). A determiner tells you, "You are at the beginning of a noun phrase." That noun phrase is going to be replaceable by *it* or *they/them/he/him*, etc.

"OK, we've covered a lot of ground today. Let's just try a few more sentences with the clause and phrase concept. We need to remember that grammar has many rules, and they're not all going to come at once. Let's be patient, and we really can grasp each one before moving on."

"Mr. Oliva, are we gonna have tests on this stuff?"

"We might. When we're ready. Now let's pull a few more sentences from *The Hobbit*. Any suggestions?"

Grammar, Day 4

To start class today, I ask the students to recall their knowledge from the last lesson. I give Sam a copy of *The Catcher in the Rye* and ask him to pull out any two sentences. This title excites the students; they've either heard of it or read it. Today I want them to understand where nouns and verbs are, relative to each other, in a sentence. On the board I write: *A subject is a noun, noun phrase, or pronoun.* While they copy this down, I scan their faces. Overall, the mood is passive, but some students wear confusion like a scar. "What I'd like to do now is search for some nouns, noun phrases, or pronouns." Searching appeals to them. "Look for *the*. When you see *the*, you're at the beginning of a noun phrase—and will soon see a noun."

Sam offers this sentence: "*The cab I had was a real old one that smelled like someone'd just tossed his cookies in it.*"

Some work with neighboring students, others alone. Corey is the first to raise his hand. "The nouns are *cab* and *cookies*," he says triumphantly. Instantly, other hands go up. I call on Erica. "What about *one*?"

I explain: "Actually, *one* is performing a special task here. It's renaming—completing—the noun *cab*.

"So it's a noun?"

"Yes, it's a noun." She smiles.

"*It* is a pronoun, right?" Alicia asks.

"Yes. Can you tell me what noun or noun phrase *it* is replacing?"

"*the cab.*"

"So then, we can see that *the cab* is a noun phrase."

Now I can tell them that *the* is a determiner, a word that signals that a noun is about to arrive. "Determiners answer the questions 'Which one?' or 'How many?' or 'Whose?' We use determiners in English to mark nouns." I write: *We always had the same meal on Saturday nights at Pencey.* Nearly every hand goes up. I call on one of the shy students: "Perry, can you tell me a determiner that is in this sentence?" When he answers with *the*, I ask him what other words might fit into that slot and be a determiner. "Well, you could put *a* there."

"You could. What else? Remember, 'Which one?' 'How many?' 'Whose?'"

I erase *the* from the board and draw a blank line, indicating that a variety of words could fit into that slot and be a determiner.

What Tom is doing here is getting students to begin to understand a key concept: slotting. The English language is a slotted system, wherein certain kinds of words can fit into certain places. Determiners can be articles (*the, a, an*), numbers and ordinals (*seven, seventh*), possessive nouns and possessive pronouns (*Judy's, her*), and demonstrative pronouns (*this, that, these, those*). The difference between adjectives and determiners, both noun modifiers, is a fuzzy area. However, the important thing to know is that both adjectives and determiners signal nouns.

So far, Tom has been teaching grammar to his "regular" ninth-grade classes. In the following journal entry, he describes teaching a grammar lesson for the first time to his tenth-grade honors students.

I'm standing by my desk after school putting off some grading, instead "planning" by shuffling papers into folders, straightening things up, tidying up my mind, when Jessica, Morgan, and Jill appear at the door. They are zealous tenth-grade honors students and their energy is inspiring, even at this point in the day. They have a youthful glow and waste no time in speaking their collective mind.

Morgan starts: "Mr. Oliva, when are we gonna do grammar?" I'm caught off guard, but I smile. These girls are serious. They want grammar and they want it now!

"We did grammar last year, but we need more," explains Jessica, one of my brightest students, with a keen sense of literary analysis and a talent for quality writing. "If we're studying essays, don't you think we should start at the beginning? I mean really look at the sentences first?" continues Morgan.

That students balk at learning grammar is a myth. Many bright students like those who visit Tom know very well that something in their education is being left out. These are competitive kids who care a great deal about their SAT and ACT test scores and who intend to apply to the nation's top colleges. They are keenly aware that grammar is important, and they are obviously confident in their ability to learn it. So here they are with their hands out.

Of course, they're right, albeit a little forward. Why haven't I integrated grammar instruction into my lessons? What am I waiting for? To be honest, I'm concerned that teaching these students grammar will leave me even more vulnerable to my own limited knowledge base. I picture myself as a dry fish flapping about on the floor in the front of the room—a subject for a head, a predicate for a tail.

"Well, um . . . you know it's hard to fit everything in what with the state exam in June and the required research paper. But we'll get to it. We'll get to it soon."

That was my impetus to decide to do a grammar lesson every Friday. Right now, I'm teaching a novel, *All Quiet on the Western Front*, with two classes and essays that stress organizational strategies with the other classes. The students should enjoy a change of pace at the end of the week—I just hope I can keep it interesting. This setup will also allow me to use authentic texts in our grammar study.

Picking out appropriate text passages proves challenging. The writing is more complex than it first appears, and I worry that students will be overwhelmed. At the same time, I see the immediate potential of studying grammar through literature. I'm hoping that doing so will change the way they look at literature. In fact, that's exactly what happens for me; while planning, I'm seeing the writing in a different way. With a mixture of confidence and trepidation, I dive in, probing the sentences for parts of speech. What I don't know I find in books or in the expertise of my colleagues. This is called learning.

After a few hours spent identifying the "perfect" passages and getting the ideas typed up, I have an activity sheet for my first Grammar Friday. It looks like this:

English 10 Honors   Mr. Oliva
Grammar

Introduction

Purpose

Grammar begins with realizing that a sentence is made of parts. Before naming these parts, you must develop an awareness of your own knowledge about the basics of grammar. Think of grammar as a Swiss Army knife. You see the different blades and tools. You will learn what each is called, what it can do, and how to use which element in different situations.

Directions

Below are excerpts from *All Quiet on the Western Front*. Divide each sentence into parts that make sense to you. It might help to know the following: A PHRASE is two or more words that stick together. Grammarians define a phrase as two or more words in sequence that form a syntactic unit that is less than a complete sentence. An example of a phrase is *in the doghouse*. A CLAUSE is a group of words that contains a subject and a predicate (verb). A simple sentence is called a simple sentence because it contains one clause. Sentences with more than one clause are called compound or complex (or compound-complex) sentences; we will learn more about these kinds of sentences later.

Passages

1. "You can see what he is thinking. There is the mean little hut on the moors, the hard work on the hearth from morning till night in the heat, the miserable pay, the dirty laborer's clothes" (Remarque 79).

2. "Towards morning, while it is still dark, there is some excitement. Through the entrance rushes in a swarm of fleeing rats that try to storm the walls. Torches light up the confusion. Everyone yells and curses and slaughters. The madness and despair of many hours unloads itself in this outburst. Faces are distorted, arms strike out, and the beasts scream; we just stop in time to avoid attacking one another" (Remarque 108).

In this simple but powerful lesson, students take the first steps toward thinking like linguistic grammarians. As Tom grows more sophisticated in his knowledge about grammar, he will be able to name the different kinds of phrases and clauses in increasingly refined ways. Once we can identify phrases and clauses, we can see how they can be expanded or condensed, moved to change where the reader's focus is going to land, replicated to produce parallel structure, and set apart from other words in the sentence by various marks of punctuation.

As students walk in, grammar gets a mixed reaction. Some students fear this stuff. (Hmmm. . . . I can relate.) Others are eager and confident. Many students immediately relate the terminology to what they've learned in their World Language classes: "Are we gonna do transitive verbs? We did those in Spanish. I know how to do those!"

I hand out the activity sheets and read over the introduction. I take some time to explain the difference between a phrase and a clause, which eases some tension. But Patricia, one of the sharpest thinkers in the room, cries out above the brewing hum: "How are we supposed to divide the sentences if we don't know grammar? I don't get the whole phrase and clause thing!"

I say: "I understand that grammar makes some of us uncomfortable. That's exactly why we're doing it. You're all at different levels, but you know a lot more than you think you do."

The students gather into naturally forming groups. I'm careful to let them find their own way. Most join up with peers on their level and begin working out a system that makes sense to them. Everybody's trying. It's an exciting atmosphere. They're making their own meaning from the task, and they have lots of questions: "Can we break the sentence after the comma?"; "Do we divide the sentence into a subject and a predicate?"; "Do you want the parts to be even?"; "Where do you put *and*?"

I keep telling them: "Just make divisions where you think the sentence breaks into parts Just form word clusters."

Forming word clusters is a fine way to begin teaching grammar because it gets students thinking syntactically. "Thinking within the sentence" is a substantial habit of mind for the student of grammar. Once you have word clusters written on the board, you can determine which are phrases and which are clauses.

If the clause can stand on its own two feet without any other words and without hitching up to any other clause, then it is an independent clause, aka a complete sentence in its own right. Clauses that need to be hitched up to another clause are called subordinate or dependent clauses. The next level would be establishing what kinds of clauses we have:

- If a clause gives information that answers the question that adjectives answer ("What kind?"), then it is an adjectival clause.
- If a clause gives information that answers the questions that adverbs answer ("Where? When? Why? To what extent? In what manner?"), then it is an adverbial clause.
- If a clause fills a slot that a noun phrase generally fills, and if it is replaceable by the word *it*, then it is a nominal.

As for phrases, we can categorize them as well. The broadest categories would be noun phrases and verb phrases.

Let's look at what Tom has accomplished. He's gotten students to see how grammar instruction is accessible and fun, that it is not about earning membership in an elite club of those who "speak correctly." He's overcome his own trepidation by beginning slowly and relying on his students' innate ability to use what they already know about grammar to bring unconscious knowledge into the conscious level so that they can advance. And he's established that first step in getting students to think like linguists: "Just form word clusters."

Once students know that grammar advancement begins with forming word clusters, they will soon be ready to name those clusters. Then they will learn how to expand and compress these clusters, to move them around, and to replicate them.

The next chapter explores the difference between the limited view of grammar instruction as a means to correct error and the wider view of it as a means for creating interesting, precise sentences.

2 Grammar as a Resource

I envision grammar instruction not as a deficit model, a cleanup kit for "finishing," but rather as a resource model, a toolbox for building. Here's the difference: If you think of grammar as a deficit model, you're thinking of it as the cleanup crew. Near the end of the project, you bring in this team of "sanitizers" and they feather-dust your prose. Grimly, they examine the writing for The Offenders. The Offenders are the commas where no commas are supposed to be and the lack of commas where commas are supposed to be. The Offenders are the subject-verb clashes and pronoun-antecedent mismatches. The Offenders are unintentional sentence fragments (or even intentional ones), the lapses in parallel syntax, the missed possessive apostrophes. In the deficit model, you are thinking of grammar *superficially*.

But if you think of grammar as a resource model, you're thinking of it as a way of understanding how you can get language to do what you want it to do. You are thinking of how you can make your language beautiful as well as functional, unobtrusive as well as powerful, efficient as well as thorough. You are thinking of grammar *rhetorically*.

Teachers who limit themselves to the deficit model risk having others play (as William Safire says) "Gotcha!" with them. If we set ourselves up and rent ourselves out as state-appointed arbiters of Truth and Justice in the English Language, we pay a dear price every time we say "It's me" or "Who are you going with?" Teachers who embrace the resource model celebrate the ever-changing nature of language and its infinite variety. The former can easily render themselves irrelevant in futile attempts to turn back the clock to some kind of imaginary Golden Age of language, where everyone spoke like Cary Grant in a Noel Coward script. Society views such teachers with sentimentality tinged with nostalgia. They are like those old-fashioned telephones that we purchase because they remind us of a more innocent time.

Linguists would call the deficit model "prescriptivism." They would call the resource model "descriptivism." Teachers who favor the former think it is their job to accept or reject language. Formal equals good; informal equals bad. Descriptivists are more like anthropologists. They make observations about how language is actually used in real communication contexts.

As English teachers, it is our job to be prescriptivist to some extent. We are tasked with inviting our students into the world of the Language of Wider Communication (LWC) (alternately called Standard English), written and spoken, and making them conversant there. To do this, we acknowledge and teach the conventions. We don't leave our students without the necessary language skills for social acceptance at all levels of society just because we are charmed by their home dialect. Within precincts such as academia, business, and broad-based social communications, it is the LWC that is expected. We have the obligation to teach our students how to read social expectations with regard to language, and how to make the necessary adjustments if that is what they choose to do for a given communicative situation. We do need to be careful how we go about doing this: "How teachers view the home language of students and their families plays a significant role in teachers' expectations and respect for students' cultures" (Perry and Delpit xiv). Disrespecting students' home language may limit students' willingness to embrace LWC. But the reality is that nonstandard dialects are simply not accepted in all social, academic, and business situations: "[M]ost teachers of . . . African-American children who have been least well-served by educational systems believe that their students' life chances will be further hampered if they do not learn Standard English. In the stratified society in which we live, they are absolutely correct" (Perry and Delpit 17).

In teaching students to code-switch in and out of the LWC, we allow them to make real choices. (By code-switching, we mean the ability to adopt the language register that suits the context. For example, when we speak to a group of parents in the auditorium, we code-switch into formal language. When we relax with our friends and family in social situations, we code-switch into colloquial language.)

Ethnic varieties of English, including African American English (AAE), flourish in colloquial speech. Everyone has a home dialect, a dialect to be used when we feel most comfortable, most emotional. That is why song lyrics in pop, country, and rhythm and blues music are treasure troves of language. Singers use the language of home and heart to declare their love, lament their losses, cry out their anthems. Likewise, authors who give their characters authentic voices use spelling, italics, and apostrophes to capture the pronunciations and cadences of English's myriad dialects.

The most important lesson we can teach our students about grammar is the importance of *listening*. And by listening, I mean more than hearing. To "listen" is to hear the music as well as the words, and to hear with the heart. The closer we listen, the more we hear variety: Language varies by region, by ethnicity, by generation, by social circumstances. Only by listening to the infinite varieties of English as linguists would, and not as pedants would, can we do what the English language itself loves to do—and that is *expand*.

As an English teacher, I've grown accustomed to the following scene: A woman sidles up to me, a smug little grin on her face. In her hand she holds a page of a text, maybe a newspaper or a memo. Displaying it before my eyes, she points to some horrifying transgression to Standard English. Perhaps it's the matching of *data* or *media* with a singular verb; perhaps it's a split infinitive. I'm expected to sigh in despair at the woeful state of the English language today. But I don't. I'm not in a state of woe. I'm in a state of *understanding that language changes*.

Here's another one: A neighbor approaches me with an inquisitive look. "Amy," he begins, "you can settle an argument that I'm having with my kids. Is *conversate* a word?" He's smiling and shaking his head in disgust in a way that lets me know he's not going to like my answer. I tell him that, well, *conversate* is a word because it conveys information that speakers of English understand. But it's a new word, an informal word, a word used colloquially in African American English, and although it hasn't gained acceptance yet in Standard English, it probably will attain full status eventually. And then I wait for the response I have come to expect: "But it's not a *word*." He has referred this controversy to a genuine, certified, bona fide English teacher to get a definitive answer, the kind of answer that English teachers are known for giving. And here I am, not giving the stamp of disapproval to an unsavory encroachment on the purity of the language. I'm only shrugging and saying: "Language varies." Who has won the argument, he or his conversating teenagers? I'm not sure he knows.

I believe that all English teachers should reflect on their own language prejudices; they should learn all they can about the nature of dialects, who speaks them, and the purposes these dialects serve in establishing communities. Our language marks us as insiders or outsiders in a particular speech community. Because each of us belongs to multiple speech communities as we go about the business and social relationships of our lives, each of us has many "language faces." As teachers, we need to understand and respect the language faces of our students and their parents. If the language faces they present at home and among their friends have features of African American English, then it behooves us to make the effort to learn about and respect those dialects. But developing an understanding of AAE and other negatively marked dialects is no less important for those who teach in schools where there are few speakers of AAE. Efforts to eradicate language prejudice through education about dialect must be in the forefront of the English teacher's sensibility, *even as we* teach the conventions of Standard English. This is what the kids call "attitude adjustment"—and what women who went to college with me called "consciousness-raising."

But the paradigm of prescriptive grammar, based as it is on "correct" and "incorrect" sentences, needs to be overhauled if we are to teach language in a way that will encourage humane and intellectually open attitudes. Linguistic grammar instruction opens students' minds to language in a way that traditional grammar instruction does not. In the next chapter, we elaborate on the difference between traditional and linguistic grammar instruction and why the latter is more natural, and easier to teach, than the former.

In "reimagining" grammar instruction as a resource model, we're actually hearkening back to the paradigm of grammar as one of the seven liberal arts (see Chapter 1). Medieval scholars believed that the value of studying the liberal arts was that such study freed (liberated) the mind to receive other learnings. In *The War against Grammar*, David Mulroy connects the classical view of grammar as a liberal art with that of Noam Chomsky and the modern linguists:

> The inclusion of grammar among the liberal arts shows that even in antiquity scholars generally sensed its kinship with logic and mathematics. Its primacy among the liberal arts reflects a fact emphasized by Aristotle: truth and falsehood can be attributed only to words organized by the rules of grammar into subjects and predicates. Not even in the privacy of one's own thoughts is it possible to conceive of a truth without at least the implicit use of grammar. (35)

I think that Mulroy has it right as he touts grammar instruction as humanizing and intellectualizing in its own right. I contrast his enlightened, positive view of the value of grammar with what I consider the wooden, utilitarian view which holds that grammar instruction is worthy only to the extent that it can be shown to "improve" writing. I put quotation marks around the word *improve* because I believe that the improvements the utilitarians recognize are measurable but shallow. These improvements are limited to surface errors in usage and mechanics: the dangling modifier that in fact does not interfere with meaning, the superfluous comma, the missing apostrophe. The improvements that Mulroy would perceive in the writing of students who have studied grammar as a liberal art would be improvements in the quality of thinking. These are less measurable, but certainly more substantive. In a posting to the listserv of the Assembly for the Teaching of English Grammar, Mulroy gives this metaphor: Two people visit the zoo. The first goes from exhibit to exhibit without knowing that all of the animals in the reptile house are called reptiles and that these reptiles share certain features. He doesn't know the names of the animals or how they are classified. The second person knows something about evolutionary lines of descent, the similarity between fishes and birds and reptiles, the structure of aquatic animals. Who has a more interesting day at the zoo?

Every complex system has terminology and taxonomy: What are the parts of the system? What do we call these parts? Where do they go and how are they related to one another? We answer these questions when we teach grammar as a resource model.

As we shift from the deficit model to the resource model, we maintain the importance of teaching students to adhere to the rules and conventions of Edited Written Standard English (EWSE), also called the Language of Wider Discourse (LWD). After all, effective communication is all about one thing: matching the message to the audience and purpose. At this time of high-stakes testing and the so-called new, so-called grammar section (really an editing section) on the SAT, we aren't going to go all wobbly on teaching the rules of punctuation and agreement. The deficit model is *part of* grammar instruction. But to limit grammar instruction to the deficit model is to miss opportunities. The deficit model doesn't open doors to deep understandings about how language works, what it can do, and how we can marshal it to our purposes.

3 Elements of Linguistic Grammar

As you read this book, you may want a resource for filling in your knowledge about the elements of linguistic grammar. You may or may not have learned the elements of English grammar in your K–12 education, in college, or in teacher training courses and graduate school. Or you may have learned traditional grammar, as I did, but you'd now like to get a more structured knowledge base about linguistic grammar. I recommend that you have a look at *Grammar Alive! A Guide for Teachers* (2003). In Chapter 8 of that book, you'll find an overview of linguistic grammar, written by Martha Kolln. I've used that information as a guide for writing this chapter.

To understand exactly what we mean by "linguistic grammar," consider what a linguist is and does. A linguist is a scholar who studies how languages are put together. A linguist finds commonalities and differences among the languages of the world. In addition to studying the lexicon (words and how they are made) and the syntax (sentences and how they are made), the linguist studies sounds, pitch, inflection, pauses, gesture, and the other features that imbue languages with meaning. Linguists are scientists. As such, they set forth hypotheses that they attempt to prove empirically and systematically. Linguists, as scientists, are nonjudgmental about language. A linguist would never wrinkle up her nose in disdain, as prescriptive grammarians are known to do, at particular accents or turns of phrase. A linguist is like a botanist who looks at all plant life objectively. A prescriptive grammarian is more like a gardener, engaging in a never-ending battle against weeds—interlopers to the garden. To the botanist, there's no such thing as a weed. Every plant has a name and a reason for growing in a particular soil under certain botanical conditions. To the linguist, every variety of language is valid and worthy of serious study.

People who think like linguistic grammarians don't think of the words in English as falling into eight parts of speech. Rather, we think of words as falling into two general classes: form-class words and structure-class words. Furthermore, we think not only of the form of grammatical elements (noun, noun phrase, prepositional phrase, etc.) but also of their function, their role in the sentence (subject, direct object, modifier, etc.). This form/structure model of word classes (traditionally called "parts of speech") is the chief difference between traditional and new grammar. That is to say, new grammarians (also called structural grammarians or linguistic grammarians) don't subscribe to the Latin-based "eight parts of speech" model of the English language. Understanding the difference between traditional and the so-called "new" grammar will require you to adapt (not erase) what you already know about traditional grammar to a new paradigm. (Of course, such adaptation will not be a problem for those who never really learned traditional grammar in the first place.) In any case, whether you are one of those people who learned traditional grammar, or whether you never learned it and it's all new to you, what follows is a map of the English language as seen through modern eyes.

I. Word Classes (Parts of Speech)

If I say "parts of speech," you are likely to conjure up the traditional eight parts of speech: noun, verb, adjective, adverb, pronoun, preposition, conjunction, interjection. You may have learned other word categories such as determiner, qualifier, and intensifier. I'll make you an offer: If you'll learn a few more parts of speech, I'll show you a way to put them all together in your brain to make them easier to handle. I'm not going to complicate your life with more terminology and categories; I'm going to simplify things by giving you a better organizational structure.

Linguistic grammarians organize parts of speech (which they call "word classes," and I will call them "word classes" from this point on) into two main groups: *form-class words* and *structure-class words*.

1. Form Classes: Nouns, Verbs, Adjectives, and Adverbs

These word classes (remember, we're now using the term *word classes* rather than *parts of speech*) are recognizable by their forms. They welcome new members, forget about some old members, and can pinch hit for one another by changing their forms. The form classes can grow in membership as we coin new words. Think of *blog, google, juicing, bling,* all new words that have signed on with the form classes of noun and/or verb.

The form class to which some words belong is not so clear. For example, the words *rain, dance,* and *smile* are just as likely to be nouns as they are to be verbs. The dictionary defines them in both ways.

Form-class words are capable of accepting affixes (prefixes and suffixes). There are two kinds of affixes, known as inflectional and derivational.

Inflectional Affixes

Inflectional affixes are suffixes that accomplish the following for nouns, verbs, adjectives, and adverbs.

The inflectional suffixes for nouns are the *-s* form that makes a noun plural and the *-s* form that makes a noun possessive. In other words, nouns can have plural and possessive forms. Although many nouns do not have plural forms (*furniture, contentment, milk, sheep, deer*), if a word can be made plural, then that word is a noun. If a word can be made possessive by adding *-s*, then that word is a noun.

To find verbs, look for the word in the sentence that can be *negated*. If a word can have an *-ing* ending, it is a verb. If a word can be signaled by auxiliaries, it is a verb. (Auxiliaries are explained in the structure-class segment that follows.)

The inflectional suffixes for verbs are *-s* (allowing the verb to agree with the third-person singular subject), *-ed* (forming the past tense of regular verbs), *-en* (forming, along with the auxiliary *have*, the past participle), and *-ing* (forming, along with the auxiliary *be*, the present participle). These are the forms of regular verbs. But the English language loves its irregular verbs, and we have some 150 of them, among them our most common verbs. You'd think irregular verbs would eventually conform to the rules, but the forms of irregular verbs are deeply embedded in the language and are Anglo-Saxon, rather than Latinate, in origin. Some irregular verbs make what we call stem changes (changes within the word itself, such as *sing-sang-sung, bring-brought-brought, take-took-taken, break-broke-broken, see-saw-seen, is-was-been*). Interestingly enough, though, every single verb in English has an *-ing* form and an *-s* form.

Verbs are systematic, having five forms:

Create: We call this the *stem*. This is how we form the infinitive.

Creates: We call this the *-s* form. This is how we form the present tense.

Created: We call this the *-ed* form. This is how we form the past tense.

Created: We call this the *-en* form. This is how we form the past participle. We use the auxiliary *have* with the past participle: *have (had) created*. Please don't be confused: We call it the *-en* even though regular verbs, like this one, use the *-ed* or *-d* suffix to form the past participle. Many words are irregular in their formation of the past participle, and many of these irregular verbs form their past participles with the *-en* ending: *take-taken, break-broken, strike-stricken*. So, for purposes of distinguishing the past participle form from the past tense, and so that we have just one way to name this form, we just call it the *-en* form.

Creating: We call this the *-ing* form. This is how we form the present participle: *is (was) creating*. We use the auxiliary *be* with the present participle.

When we speak of a word class as being *systematic*, what we mean is that the words in that class form reliable patterns in how they change forms. We've just seen how regular verbs are very systematic. Irregular verbs are said to be less systematic because they change their forms in less consistent ways.

Now we can talk about adjectives. Adjectives are less systematic than verbs, but most one-syllable adjectives can accept the *-er*/*-est* endings to express comparative and superlative degree, respectively. Adjectives of more than one syllable generally use *more* and *most* to express comparative and superlative degree. That is not to say, however, that all adjectives can be "degree-ified." Examples of such "non-degree-bearing" adjectives are *main*, *principal*, *former*, *potential*, and *atomic* (Haussamen, *Grammar Alive!* 82).

Like nouns, adjectives can undergo functional shifts, as in these examples, in which words we generally think of as adjectives are filling nominal (noun) functions:

Only the *strong* survive.

The *rich* are different.

The land of the *free* and the home of the *brave*.

Derivational Affixes

Speaking of functional shifts, now would be a good point at which to talk about derivational affixes. Although the term sounds formidable and abstract (at least, it did to me until I came to understand it, which took a while), derivational affixes are easy to understand. Simply stated, they are the prefixes and suffixes that morph a word into another word class (part of speech) or, in some cases, change the meaning: *boy/boyhood*; *friend/friendship*. They are prefixes and suffixes that formalize a functional shift. In the functional shifts we saw earlier (*the <u>rich</u> are different*), the word itself did not change form:

I'll <u>bag</u> my own groceries, thank you. And I'll <u>bottle</u> my own water.
I'll <u>box</u> up my belongings and <u>book</u> myself a flight out of town.*

---

*These examples are like *rain* and *dance*, etc.—words that are both nouns and verbs. We can use many nouns as verbs, complete with verb inflections, so they become verbs. These are not in the same category as either *boy* + *ish* or *boy* + *hood*.

But when a word changes its form by adding a prefix or a suffix in order to slip into the skin of another part of speech, we call that prefix or suffix a derivational affix.

Here are some derivational affixes that create nouns: *-tion, -ment, -ness, -ance, -ence, -al, -age, -er, -itude, -ry, -ity*. Some that create verbs are *-ify, -en, en-, -ate, -ize*. Some that create adjectives are *-ous, -y, -ful, -ate, -ish, -ary, -ive, -able, -ible, -able*. And the famous transformer of adjectives into adverbs is *-ly*. Students enjoy wordplay in which they create never-before-seen words through derivational affixes, wherein the process of blending a banana into a vanilla shake is *bananafication,* with the resulting flavor being described as *bananalilla.*

2. Structure Classes: Determiners, Auxiliaries, Qualifiers, Prepositions, Particles, Conjunctions, Pronouns

Words belonging to the structure classes don't often accept new members. For this reason, we call them the *closed* classes. If the English language were a suit of clothing, the form-class words would be the fabric and accessories; the structure-class words would be the thread, buttons, zippers, and hooks that hold the garment together but don't attract much notice when they're doing their jobs. Take a common sentence:

Jack and Jill went up the hill to fetch a pail of water.

If your structure-class words don't show up for work one day, the sentence looks like this:

Jack Jill went hill fetch pail water.

Although you have all of the information you need to understand what is happening, what you don't have is a sentence that sounds like English. That is because the structure-class words, aside from the meaning they add, provide the rhythm of the English language. Most structure-class words are unstressed. As such, their lowered pitch creates the valleys in the cadence of language. For native speakers, this up-and-down rhythm operates below the conscious awareness; however, English language learners find the structure classes very difficult to master. English language learners may need explicit teaching in creating the rhythms of English.

Following is an explanation of the different kinds of structure-class words.

Determiners: Here comes a noun!

Determiners signal nouns. When you see *the, a,* or *an,* you can be certain that a noun phrase is being started. *The, a,* and *an* are determiners called *articles*. Their sole purpose in life is to signal nouns. But there are other kinds of determiners; one kind of determiner is the possessive pronoun: *my, her, his, their, our, your*. For that matter, any kind of possessive (*Veronica's room*) is a determiner because it signals a noun. Demonstrative pronouns—*this, that, these,* and *those*—are determiners, as are the indefinite pronouns, such as *some, many, each, every,* and *all*. And the cardinal numbers (*one, two . . .*) as well as the ordinal numbers (*first, second, third . . .*) are determiners too. Determiners are signalers of nouns. Determiners of this kind do not have syntactic flexibility. That is, they can't change their forms by adding suffixes, the way an adjective (*green, greener, greenest*) can.

When native speakers of English learn another language, they may have to get used to the masculinity and femininity of nouns and the concordant masculinity or femininity of determiners in the target language. In Spanish, that would be *la* or *el*. Native speakers of English produce definite or indefinite articles (*the*, or *a/an*, respectively) without thinking. But, as you may have noticed, English language learners, who have to construct knowledge about features of the language that native speakers learn naturally, need to be taught explicitly to use *the*, *a*, or *an*.

Conscious knowledge of determiners, how they work, and what they are capable of doing can make us more careful writers. The absence or presence of a determiner can change meaning, as in *Few people attended the meeting* and *A few people attended the meeting*. Writers can and should take advantage of the determiner's ability to link new information to previously given information, leading off not only sentences but also paragraphs with noun determiners:

> <u>These</u> details were instrumental in our overall understanding of the situation.

> <u>This</u> reaction was expected.

It is important to distinguish determiners from adjectives and other noun modifiers. Determiners help guide the reader into noun phrase territory. Knowing where noun phrases begin is an important concept in understanding English grammatical patterns.

Auxiliaries

Auxiliaries are often called helping verbs, and you probably learned them as belonging to the verb class rather than as their own word class, as we are presenting them here. We speak of three classes of auxiliaries.

i. Have and Be. *Have* and *be* form the perfect (*have worked*) and progressive (*is working*) forms of verbs, respectively. *Have* and *be* can also operate in tandem, as in *have been working*. *Have* and *be* get jobs as verbs in their own right. (*I have a job. I am a doll doctor.*) So they are members of both the verb class and the auxiliary class. *Be* also produces the passive voice when teamed up with the past participle: *was written; is told*.

ii. Modal Auxiliaries. *Will, shall, can, could, should, would, may, might, must*. We use these modal auxiliaries when we want to express that the action of a verb did not actually occur: *We should leave soon. We should have left long ago. Well, I guess we should be leaving now.* Note that in these examples, we're still hanging around! We haven't actually done the action of leaving. We're just speculating on what we *will, shall, can, could, should, would, may, might, must* do—not actually doing it.

iii. Do. *Do* is a special auxiliary that has several jobs, which it performs when no other auxiliary is present: forming questions (*Do you think I'm sexy?*); creating a negative (*No, I do not think so.*); creating a tag question (*You live in New Jersey, don't you?*); adding emphasis (*I did tell you that I would be home late.*). Finally, *do* is sometimes a verb in its own right: *He does well in algebra.*

Considering auxiliaries as a separate word class is one of the ways in which linguists differ from traditional grammarians. But, when you understand that linguists view verbs as words that can take an *-s* and an *-ing* form, you'll understand why auxiliaries such as *can, must, could, may,* and *might* are in a class by themselves. Another difference between auxiliaries and verbs is that verbs belong to the form class, as they can easily morph into nouns or even adjectives. But auxiliaries, members of the structure class, cannot morph into nouns or other parts of speech.

Qualifiers

Qualifiers, classified as adverbs by traditional grammarians, answer the question *To what extent?* They signal adjectives and some adverbs (*very big, very slowly*).

Prepositions

Prepositions are easy to identify. A *preposition* is a word that combines with a nominal (the object of the preposition) to form a phrase that we call a prepositional phrase. A prepositional phrase functions adverbially, as a verb modifier (answering the questions that adverbs answer: *when? where? why? in what manner? to what extent?*), or adjectivally, as the modifier of a noun (answering the questions that adjectives answer: *what kind? which one?*).

Many teachers favor the "bee and the flower" visual: Picture a bee. Picture a flower. Now fill in this sentence to show where the bee flies, relative to the flower: *under, over, around, through, inside, outside,* etc.

Lists of prepositions are easy to find, and many people like to tell me that they learned the list by singing them to the tune of "Yankee Doodle Dandy" or some such. The trouble with that approach to learning prepositions is that it doesn't have a grammatical base, and so the learner is likely to end up confusing prepositions with other small, common words.

The most common prepositions—*of, in, on, at, for, with*—are good to have handy, even posted in the classroom, because they provide dimension in sentences and are great for adding detail to content area writing. Once students develop awareness of prepositional phrases, they can consciously use them not only to add dimension and detail but also to vary their sentence structure by beginning some sentences with prepositional phrases.

Students should also be aware of phrasal prepositions: *instead of, inside of, outside of, according to, with regard to, because of,* etc.

Particles

A particle is a word, often a preposition, that hitches on to a verb to make it what we call a phrasal verb. Examples of phrasal verbs, with their particles underlined, are *try on, break up, break out, break down, step up, step out, call off, call up, call in, call out.* Such phrasal verbs come to mean more than the sum of their parts. The resulting phrase does not retain the literal meaning of the two words added together, but instead takes on a whole new meaning. Phrasal verbs, used lavishly in conversation, are particularly vexing for English language learners who are using a pocket dictionary to improve their English skills. Pocket dictionaries aren't much help with phrasal verbs. (Case in point: *Look up,* as in "to consult a reference source," is a phrasal verb. It differs from the literal meaning of *look up,* as in "Raise your eyes to the heavens.")

Teaching about phrasal verbs offers a convenient transition into vocabulary elevation because the phrasal verb represents the informal way of expressing an idea that the more formal Latinate word expresses:

Turn down = reject

Call off = cancel

Tune out = disengage

Speed up = accelerate

Conjunctions

Conjunctions are the joining devices of grammar. Like the joining devices in the hardware store, the choice depends on what they're connecting and why.

Coordinating Conjunctions. Coordinating conjunctions are capable of joining equal elements, both complete sentences and structures within the sentence. The most common ones are *and, but, so, yet, or,* and *nor.*

Subordinating Conjunctions. Subordinating conjunctions are capable of hitching up a subordinating (aka dependent) clause to a main clause, thus forming a complex sentence. Some common subordinating conjunctions are *after, if, since, because, although,* and *even though.* (If you noticed that *after* can also function as a preposition, then you're doing great! When we say *After we dined, we divvied up the check,* we have a subordinating conjunction because *After we dined* is a clause; when we say *After dinner, we divvied up the check,* then we have a prepositional phrase, with *dinner* as the object of the preposition *after.*)

Correlative Conjunctions. Correlative conjunctions are paired joiners: *both-and, not only-but also, either-or, neither-nor.* Correlative conjunctions add a dash of sophistication to a writer's style. The most common of them, *both-and,* connects only structures within the sentence; the others can connect both full sentences and their parts.

Conjunctive Adverbs. Conjunctive adverbs, as the name indicates, do double duty: both joining sentences and providing adverbial information (*when? where? how? why? to what extent?*). The best known conjunctive adverbs are *however, therefore, nevertheless,* and *moreover.*

Pronouns

As we've seen, many pronouns go out to work as other word classes in function while remaining pronouns in form. You've undoubtedly heard it said that a pronoun "replaces a noun." Actually, what a pronoun replaces is not a noun but a nominal: that is, a noun, a noun phrase (noun plus its modifiers), a verb phrase acting nominally, or a noun clause (subject-verb structure doing the work of a noun). For example:

<u>The first three chapters in this book</u> contain <u>information about linguistic grammar.</u>

They   it

<u>*Keeping up with the Jones's*</u> is impossible.

It

Later in this chapter, we say more about nominals.

Pronouns break into several categories. We have the personal pronouns (*I, me, it, you, my, your*, etc.), indefinite pronouns (*every, everyone, many, any*, etc.), relative pronouns (*who, whose, whom, that, which*), reflexive pronouns (*myself, yourself, himself*, etc.), and demonstrative pronouns (*this, that, these, those*).

II. Form and Function   People in the subj.

We've seen how words in the four form classes (nouns, verbs, adjectives, and adverbs) can shape themselves into different forms. Now we'll see why a word might want to do that. The *form* of a word is one thing; its *function* is another. By *function*, we mean "the job that the word performs in its sentence."

Let's take the sentence *Cinderella tested the slipper*. The words belonging to the form classes are *Cinderella, tested*, and *slipper*: two nouns, one proper noun and one noun that is derived from a verb (*to slip*), and one verb in the past tense (*tested*). Let's add a few more form-class words to this sentence: *Cinderella, the future spouse of the prince, confidently tested her own slipper*. Table 3.1 shows how derivational affixes are capable of changing the form class of the words in this sentence.

If you are used to traditional grammar, you may not be thinking in terms of form and function. When we speak of a word's *form*, we refer to the way that word is used in its original, or usual, way. The word *card*, for example is a noun in form. But *card* can morph in function to an adjective, as in *a card table*. And *card* can even function as a verb, as in the slogan *We Card*, meaning "We check your ID card to verify your age." In matters other than language, we commonly think in terms of form and function. My bedroom door sometimes locks itself of its own accord, forcing me to do some creative thinking as to how I'm going to gain access without having to call in professional help. I've learned that I can simply stretch out a paper clip, stick the end of it into the lock mechanism, and suddenly the doorknob turns. I don't know how many of our students remember the television series *MacGyver*, but you probably do. In every episode, the hero would cleverly get himself out of a jam and beat a ticking bomb by coming up with an ingenious use for a common object, demonstrating the meaning of the term *functional shift*. In grammar, a functional shift is the deployment of a word into a part of speech that we don't normally associate with its form.

Table 3.1. How form-class words change form.

Word as Used Here	How This Word Can Change Its Form (and Function)
Cinderella (here used as a proper noun)	Cinderella (adjective, as in *Her life was like a Cinderella story*)
Future (here used as an adjective, modifying *spouse*)	Future (used as noun, as in *the future*) Futures (pluralized noun) Futuristic (adjective, as in *futuristic vision*)
Spouse (here used as a noun)	Spouses (pluralized noun) Spousal (adjective, as in *spousal support*)
Prince (here used as a noun)	Princes (pluralized noun) Princely (adjective, as in *princely duties*) Note: Please don't be confused by the fact that the *-ly* suffix here forms an adjective and not an adverb. Other *-ly* adjectives are *friendly*, *lovely*, and *wifely*. The *-ly* adverbs are formed by adding *-ly* to adjectives, not to nouns.
Confidently (here used as an adverb)	Confident (adjective, as *confident smile*) Confidence (noun, as in *the confidence*) Confidences (pluralized noun) Confidential (adjective, as in *confidential information*) Confidentially (adverb, as in *confidentially revealed*)
Tested	Test, tests, tested, testing (other forms of the verb) Test (noun, as in *the test*) Tests (pluralized noun, as in *many tests*)
Slipper (here used as a noun)	Slip, slipped, slipping (other forms of the verb) Slippers (pluralized noun) Slippery (adjective, as in *slippery slope*)

III. Sentence Constituents

Sentence constituents are the parts of the sentence:

> Sentence = Noun Phrase + Verb Phrase

The function of the noun phrase is to be the subject (and noun phrases perform other functions, as we'll see); the function of the verb phrase is to be the predicate. We'll talk about the noun phrase and the verb phrase individually.

Phrases and Clauses

Students need to understand the difference between a phrase and a clause and between a clause and a sentence. Give them opportunities to divide sentences into parts, deciding which words belong together as word clusters. Once they get a feel for how a sentence consists of constituent parts, you can begin talking about noun phrases and verb phrases. Much of linguistic grammar is about thinking in terms of phrases rather than a list of single words.

You may not be used to the terms *noun phrase* and *verb phrase*. These terms are used by linguists and are not usually used by traditional grammarians. A phrase is a word or group of words functioning as a unit within the sentence: That is, most phrases are word clusters, but the noun functioning as the subject or direct object, for example, can be a single word, such as *Joe* or *they*. A phrase is a word cluster that does not have both a subject and a verb. Once the word cluster has both a subject and a verb, it morphs into a clause. If the clause can stand alone as a complete sentence, we call it an independent clause. If the clause must be attached to another clause in order to form a complete sentence, we call it a subordinate, or a dependent, clause. The independent clause to which the subordinate clause is attached is called the main clause. A sentence consisting of two independent clauses joined together (by either a semicolon or a comma and a coordinating conjunction) is called a compound sentence. A sentence consisting of a main clause and a dependent clause is called a complex sentence. And a sentence consisting of two or more independent clauses and one or more dependent clauses is called a compound-complex sentence.

The Noun Phrase

I want you to understand three things about noun phrases:

1. A noun phrase, often signaled by a determiner, is replaceable by a pronoun. That is, you can pull out the noun phrase and replace it with a pronoun such as *it*, *she*, or *they*.

2. A noun phrase is expandable in various ways.

3. A noun phrase operates as a unit in the sentence and can fill seven roles: subject, direct object, indirect object, object complement, predicate noun, appositive, object of a preposition.

Noun Phrase Borders. The noun phrase is replaceable by the pronoun *it*, if singular; *they*, if plural; *he* or *she* if a person or animal (or by *them*, *him*, or *her* if the noun phrase is functioning as an object). The first word of a noun phrase is likely to be a noun determiner, as previously explained. The chief noun of the noun phrase is called its headword. The headword may be the final word in the noun phrase: *a cozy little cottage*. If you include a prepositional phrase as a modifier, it follows the headword: *a cozy little cottage by the sea*. You can even have multiple prepositional phrases: *the cozy little cottage by the sea on a breezy lane*. In fact, you can even have a whole clause introduced by a relative pronoun (thus being called a relative clause) following the headword: *the cozy little cottage, which I used to visit*. Note that the pronoun *it* can replace the entire structure, regardless of its complexity: *The cozy little cottage by the sea on a breezy lane, which I used to visit, has fallen into disrepair*; *It has fallen into disrepair*.

Noun Phrase Expansion. As you've seen in the preceding example, a noun phrase can be expanded in either direction of the headword. We have a systematic way of building a noun phrase. We can add adjectives or nouns to the pre-headword position. The adjective must go first, then the noun:

the brown grocery <u>bag</u>

We can add a participle. A participle is a verb in form: The *-ing* form is called the present participle; the *-en* form is called the past participle.

the wrinkled brown grocery bag

And we can multiply any of these kinds of adjectives, but we have to follow the pattern. Note that a comma separates adjectives that could have the word *and* between them. In the sentence *The funny little clown*, you could not interpose *and* between *funny little* with *and*; but if those adjectives were, say, *clumsy* and *inexperienced*, you would place a comma between them. You can also use the test that if adjectives can reverse their order in the sentence, they need a comma between them.

Following the headword, in what we call the post-headword position, we can modify with a prepositional phrase, or even multiple prepositional phrases:

the <u>bag</u> with the hole in the bottom

We can even expand the noun phrase by adding an entire relative clause. That relative clause, because it is doing adjective work, is called an adjectival clause:

the bag that I found in the garage

Adjectivals. What I want you to see here is that noun modifiers are not limited to adjectives, nor are modifiers limited to the pre-noun position. When an element whose form is, say, a noun or a prepositional phrase or a relative clause is functioning the way an adjective functions, we call that element an *adjectival* because its function is that of an adjective (noun modifier) even though it is not a single word. An adjective is a single word, belonging to the form class. An adjectival is an adjective or any other word or word group that is functioning as a noun modifier. The difference between an adjective and an adjectival is the difference between form (adjective) and function (adjectival).

Here's an example of a sentence that has three adjectivals in it:

The *brick* house *that the third little pig built* was *very sturdy.*

Note that *that the third little pig built* answers the question *which one?* to the word *house.* Note also that *brick* answers the question *what kind?* to the word *house*, and *very sturdy* further describes the house.

Nominals. We can refer to any word or group of words that functions in the way a noun phrase functions as a *nominal.* A nominal can be a single noun, a noun phrase, a noun clause, a pronoun, or even another kind of word class that is fulfilling one of the seven roles a nominal can fill (see the following list). In the sentence *Only the strong survive*, the word *strong*, though an adjective in form, is functioning as a nominal. It is part of the noun phrase *only the strong.* In the sentence *Only those who can leap tall buildings in a single bound survive*, the words *those who can leap tall buildings in a single bound* form a nominal. Be not afear'd of nominals. You can easily identify them simply by asking yourself which word(s) in the sentence can be replaced by a pronoun. The difference between a noun and a nominal is the difference between form (noun) and function (nominal). Let's see what our grocery bag can do.

Seven Roles That a Nominal Can Fill

Subject: *A grocery bag* makes a great book cover.

Direct object: I found *a grocery bag.*

Indirect object: I showed *a grocery bag* to the clerk.

Subject complement: This is *a grocery bag.*

Object complement: I consider this thing *a grocery bag*.

Object of preposition: I put my books inside *a grocery bag*.

Appositive: One thing, *a grocery bag*, was in my hands when I fell.

What are the practical applications of being able to identify noun phrases? Students who understand the expandability and versatility of noun phrases have a great deal of control over their sentences: They may be able to add detail and variety; they may be able to spot redundancy and tighten up a flabby noun phrase. As readers, they can learn to read words in clusters, a very important meaning-making habit of mind. In *Hamlet*, Claudius remarks that when sorrows come, they come not in single spies, but in battalions. Well, when meaning is formed, it is formed not in single words but in phrases. It's important to be able to read noun phrases as units, units that are capable of fulfilling various roles within the sentence.

Adverbials. By now, you should be expecting me to establish the same relationship between adverbs and adverbials as I did with nouns and nominals, adjectives and adjectivals. And that is exactly how it is: An adverb is a single word, a member of the form class, that adds information of time, place, reason, etc., to the verb. It answers the questions *where? when? why? to what extent? how?* Adverbials are structures that provide this information. For example, in the sentence *Cinderella's feet ached when she wore her glass slippers*, the clause *when she wore her glass slippers* is an adverbial clause because it contains a subject and a verb (making it a clause), is introduced by the subordinating conjunction *when*, and tells *when*. The difference between an adverb and an adverbial is the difference between form (adverb) and function (adverbial).

Specialized Phrases: Movable Participles, Movable Adjectives, Appositives, Absolute Phrases. Now we can move beyond the basics:

The chick, having learned how to fly, left the nest.

Having learned how to fly, the chick left the nest.

The chick left the nest, having learned how to fly.

Having learned how to fly is a participial phrase that is an expansion of the noun phrase *the chick*. The home base of this participial phrase is after the headword, as you see it placed in the first example above. This participial phrase is movable because (1) it modifies the subject and (2) it is nonrestrictive. By *nonrestrictive*, we mean that it comments on—it does not define—the noun that it modifies. Nonrestrictive modifiers are set off by commas, making them appear parenthetical. Some people use the term *nonessential* instead of *nonrestrictive*. When we say "doesn't define" or "nonessential," we mean that the noun headword is clear to the reader without that information.

These are participial phrases and, as you can see, they are movable within the sentence. A participle is that form of a verb that goes with the auxiliary *have* or *be*, as in

The clock has broken. The clock is breaking.

But a participle can be used not only as a verb but also as an adjective:

The broken clock

The breaking heart

Such adjectives have special powers because they are made out of verbs. But, as we saw in the earlier example, we can do fancy things with participles. We can make them into phrases that are movable within the sentence, thus creating special effects:

The runner, nearly tripping on her shoelace, stole second.

The runner stole second, nearly tripping on her shoelace.

Nearly tripping on her shoelace, the runner stole second.

But note, please, that such elements are movable only if they modify the subject. Otherwise, they create ambiguity and are known as dangling modifiers. Here's an example:

Wrapped in tinfoil, Sam thought the grilled tuna sandwich was a welcome change from the usual peanut butter and jelly.

It is obviously supposed to be the grilled tuna sandwich, not Sam, that is wrapped in tinfoil. A possible revision would have the sandwich becoming the subject:

Wrapped in tinfoil, the grilled tuna sandwich was delicious and, Sam thought, a welcome change from the usual peanut butter and jelly.

We can draw special attention to adjectives by placing them in the post-noun position and setting them off with commas:

The new girl, a little shy, stood in the doorway.

Cassius, lean and hungry, looks like a man who thinks too much.

Appositives are nominals, usually noun phrases, that are often set off by commas. Appositives rename another noun:

Appositives, <u>nominals that are set off by commas</u>, rename another noun.

Lombard Street, <u>the crookedest street in the world</u>, is a famous San Francisco tourist attraction.

My dog, <u>an Australian shepherd</u>, loves to fetch sticks.

Arguably the most sophisticated of the special effects noun phrases, the absolute phrase contains a single post-noun modifier, often a participle. The absolute phrase modifies the sentence as a whole. It is often called a free modifier. Here's an example:

My high school English notebook, <u>its pages yellowing</u>, is a resource I still consult.

<u>Arms outstretched</u>, the baby expected to be taken out of her crib.

He looked at me in surprise, <u>his brows raised</u>.

We can say that these special effect noun phrases act as zoom lenses, focusing the reader on particular details.

As you can see, there's a lot to learn about noun phrases. They are elemental in the English language, and getting a sense of their possibilities is certainly a major part of learning the craft of writing. Start opening your eyes to the noun phrases in the literature you teach, and soon you will be able to open your students' eyes to them. The next step will be for students to begin using noun phrases consciously in new ways. This awareness will make them not only better writers but also more careful readers.

Being a careful reader means knowing when the writer intends for you to slow down. When sentences are crafted with special effects, as with post-noun placements set off by commas, the reader is being directed to linger. That is why such sentences are found in literary text, both fiction and nonfiction.

The Verb Phrase

When describing the sentence as "noun phrase plus verb phrase," by *verb phrase* we generally mean the predicate (but, as clarified below, we can also be referring to structures used as adjectivals [participial phrases], nominals [gerund phrases], and adverbials; these last three functions can be carried out by verb phrases that are infinitive phrases in form). We have three kinds of verbs: *linking*, *intransitive*, and *transitive*. Of these three, the only one requiring nothing but the subject and the verb—the two-word sentence—is the intransitive verb: *It rained. Stuff happens. Teenagers giggle.* Linking verbs require subject complements to complete the sentence: *I am a teacher. Dry ice is hot. Apple pie smells delicious. He looks strange.* Transitive verbs require direct objects to complete the sentence: *Everybody loves Raymond. Hamlet saw the ghost.*

But verb phrases are often found in off-duty capacities as well. Earlier we spoke of the participle that acts not as a verb but as an adjective: *a galloping horse*. There are two other kinds of off-duty verbs: gerunds and infinitives. We call these participles, gerunds, and infinitives *verbals*. A gerund is an *-ing* verb that functions as a noun: *Singing in the shower is my favorite pastime*. An infinitive combines *to* with the uninflected (stem) form of the verb. It can function as a nominal (doing what noun phrases do): *To know her is to love her*; or as an adverbial (doing what adverbs do): *I called you to find out the homework*; or as an adjectival (doing what adjectives do): *We were the last to get the news*.

To expand the verb phrase, think in terms of describing the action with adverbials. Think in terms of answering the kinds of questions that adverbs answer: *when? where? why? to what extent? in what manner?*

Between the Noun Phrase and the Verb Phrase: Opportunity

Between the noun phrase and the verb phrase is a place where there can be a pause. In that space, we can insert modifying elements, setting them off by a pair of commas. *My dad comes up with really clever practical jokes* becomes *My dad, when he puts his mind to it, comes up with really clever practical jokes*.

The same pause of opportunity for modification exists between the verb and the direct object: *Everybody loves, at one time or another, someone*.

IV. Sentence Patterns

We close this chapter with the eight major patterns of sentences in the English language. When your students understand these patterns, they will have the underpinnings of grammar, the basics on which to elaborate or condense so as to produce clear, concise, interesting sentences. The sentence patterns are categorized in accordance with what their verb phrases require. Every sentence has a subject, and every sentence has a verb, but the demands of the verb define the pattern.

The sentence patterns fall into two divisions: action verbs and linking verbs. The action verb patterns subdivide into two types: intransitive verbs and transitive verbs. Intransitive verbs require no further information to complete the sentence, thereby consisting of only two required slots: subject and verb. This is the only one of the seven patterns having only two required slots. Transitive verbs split into three patterns: those that take direct objects only, those that take indirect objects, and those that take object complements. Object complements can be adjectival or nominal. The diagrams in Figures 3.1–3.5 illustrate the five action verb patterns.

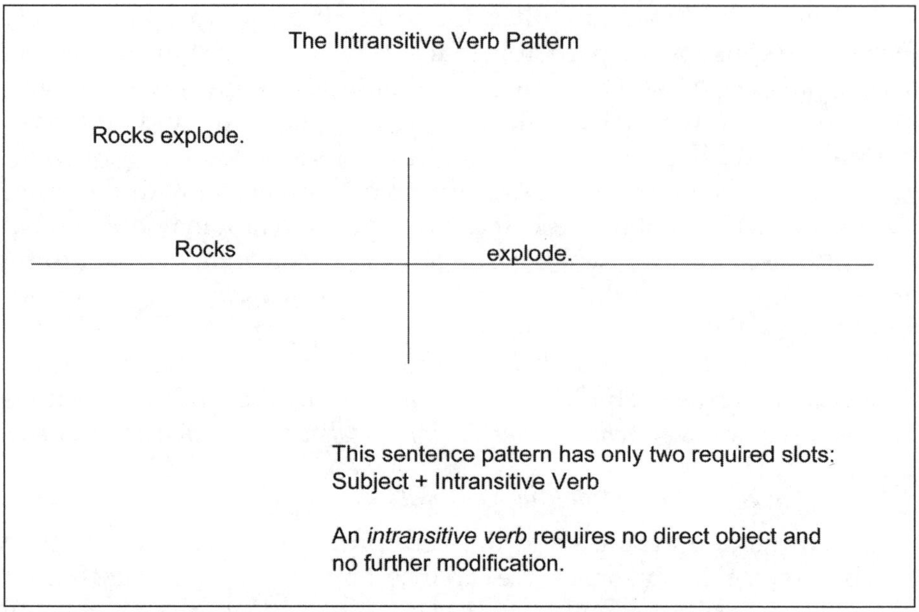

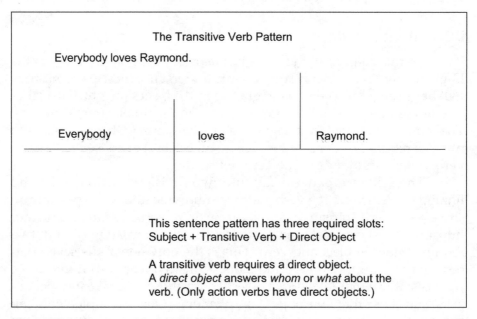

The Intransitive Verb Pattern

Rocks explode.

Rocks | explode.

This sentence pattern has only two required slots:
Subject + Intransitive Verb

An *intransitive verb* requires no direct object and
no further modification.

Figure 3.1. The intransitive verb pattern.

The Transitive Verb Pattern

Everybody loves Raymond.

Everybody | loves | Raymond.

This sentence pattern has three required slots:
Subject + Transitive Verb + Direct Object

A transitive verb requires a direct object.
A *direct object* answers *whom* or *what* about the
verb. (Only action verbs have direct objects.)

Figure 3.2. The transitive verb pattern.

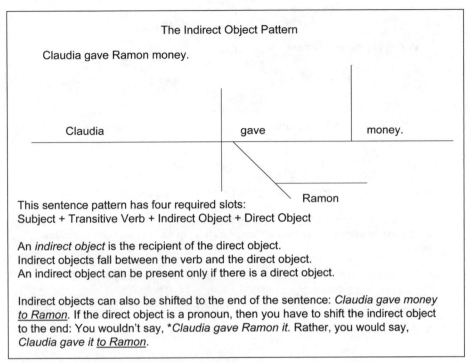

Figure 3.3. The indirect object pattern.

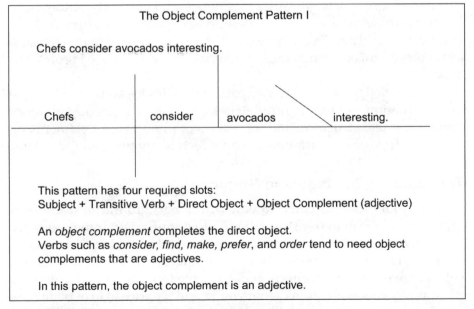

Figure 3.4. The object complement pattern I.

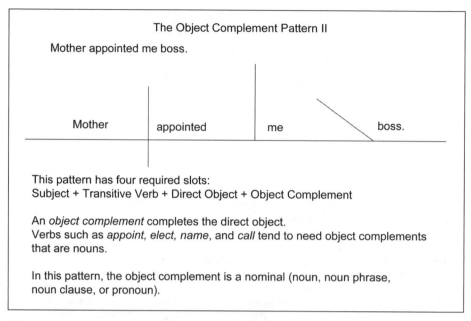

Figure 3.5. The object complement pattern II.

Linking verbs require a subject complement. A subject complement serves to rename (if it is a nominal) or describe (if it is an adjectival) the subject. The major difference between action verb patterns and
linking verb patterns is that, with action verb patterns, the direct object
is *different from the subject*, whereas in the linking verb patterns, the subject complement either renames or describes the subject (see Figures 3.6–
3.8).

Knowledge of the sentence patterns facilitates an understanding
of punctuation, sentence completeness, stylistic fragments, sentence
variety, parallel structure, and the effects of placement of elements on
meaning. It serves as a framework on which to organize all the details.

Transitioning to Linguistic Grammar

What if your students come to you with a background in traditional
grammar? For you to transition them into linguistic grammar, they are
not going to have to unlearn anything. You will be taking their knowledge to the next level by speaking of form, function, and frames. All
subject areas have ambiguous and refinable terminology: If you were
teaching social studies, think what you would have to do to explain how
words like *conservative* and *liberal* change with context. Think of your

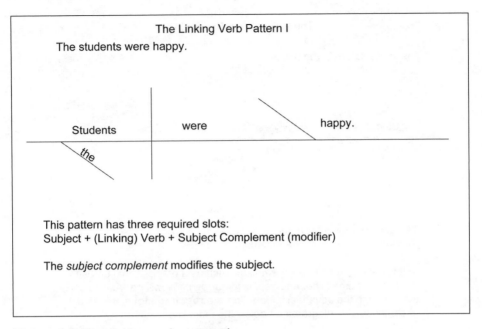

Figure 3.6. The linking verb pattern I.

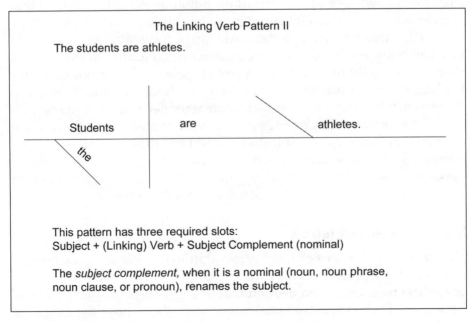

Figure 3.7. The linking verb pattern II.

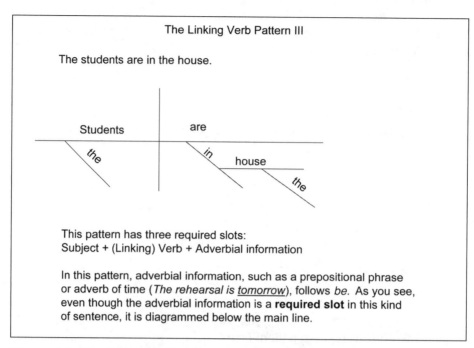

Figure 3.8. The linking verb pattern III.

students' knowledge of traditional grammar as prior knowledge that you can build on with your instruction in linguistic grammar, rather than knowledge that has to be "unlearned." But expect students to come to you with varying degrees of exposure to formal grammar instruction. With the mobility of society, with private schools being notorious for teaching grammar, our students do not form a homogeneous body when it comes to what they know about grammar (or geography or mathematics, for that matter). Rely on the vast—indeed, the astonishing—amount of grammar they do know intuitively, and trust that you can refine that intuitive knowledge into explicit knowledge that can be put to use to make your students better at communication and at understanding other languages, dialects, and cultures, as well as their own.

Instructional Strategies

The information in this chapter is foundational. Your students need to have this information in order for you to proceed with discussions of usage and mechanics and beyond that to the rhetorical effects that can be achieved when we can speak accurately about how the language works. You don't have to "take time out" of your instruction in authentic language and literature experiences to teach these fundamentals. Grammar instruction and literary-rhetorical instruction can occupy the same space. Here's how:

1. The literature that your students are already reading has all the examples you need to illustrate the concepts of grammar.

2. The writing that your students are already doing offers endless opportunities for phrase expansion, parallel structure, rhetorical placements, functional shifting.

3. You are teaching punctuation anyway. Punctuation rules follow grammatical contours. You need to use grammatical language to teach punctuation effectively.

4. If you teach the parts of speech as I've done here, using frames, students learn them much faster than they will if you go back to traditional (abstract) definitions.

TEACHER'S JOURNAL: SENTENCE PATTERNS

I'd be remiss if I didn't mention the ambiguities inherent in the teaching of grammar. In fact, that's really what this is all about: how we, as teachers, can transfer our own anxieties if we're teaching something we feel insecure about. In almost every lesson I taught, the intricacies of grammar reared up like tractor trailers tailgating in a rearview mirror. But rather than let them scare me, I pushed on, admitting my uncertainty, and using these moments as lessons in humility: moments to illuminate my own love of learning for my students.

In cases where my limited expertise was exposed, I remained honest and curious. I assured the students that I would find the answers swiftly by consulting texts and colleagues. In most cases, the students were kind and appreciative, eager to see their teacher do the hunting he so often asked of them. Simply put: Uncertainty proved a valuable vehicle for practicing what I preach. My lesson on sentence patterns illustrates this paradigm well.

My tenth-grade honors students are immersed in the daunting novel *The Scarlet Letter*. Thanks to our grammar lessons and a healthy dose of close reading techniques, Hawthorne's phrases, once imposing, are now coming alive. The students are keeping dialectical journals (personal and analytical written conversations about the specific language and elements of the text). Using a PowerPoint presentation developed by Amy Benjamin on sentence patterns, I give them a chance to explore the characterization in the novel, simultaneously informing their reading and their journals.

I want the room to feel alive today. Because I'm using an LCD projector (teachers without access to this technology could easily print out the presentation) to project the PowerPoint onto a screen, the lights are off when my classes enter. To counter conditions that can sometimes produce a sleepy mood, I have Count Basie's "Jumpin' at the Woodside" slicing through the dark stillness. Grammar lessons are now associated with fun; my students enter excited by the vibe. As she enters, Alison exclaims, "We're doing grammar today!" It's a far cry from the dismay normally associated with the subject, and I couldn't be happier.

I expect this lesson to be easy to teach. I'm hooked up to the Internet, where I've located Amy's slide show titled "My Big Fat Grammar Project" via her website. The students like the title. As I begin, Ryan murmurs to Phil sitting next to him, "I like doing grammar more than *The Scarlet Letter.*" What he hasn't realized is that we're covering both, combining our study of the text with our study of language.

To begin, I explain, "Today we're going to look at the basic sentence patterns to illuminate more about what you already know about grammar. It's difficult to talk about language without knowing the names of its parts. Once you know and understand the names, things like *transitive verbs* versus *intransitive verbs*, *direct objects*, *indirect objects*, and *object complements*, you can discuss, write, and even think more effectively about language. Look at it this way: You go to your local Home Depot in need of some tools. If you don't know what to ask for, it's going to be a tough trip. Do you need nails or screws? A Phillips head or a flat screwdriver? Communication about any system requires knowledge of the names of its parts. Similarly, you need to be informed about the terms associated with grammar and language. To do this, we'll view a little show that focuses on clear examples of each pattern. Take notes in the grammar section of your notebook, and be sure to leave space for your own creative sentences." I click on the first slide.

I ask the students to copy the diagram into their notebooks, careful to give them adequate time. It reads, "The Action Verb Patterns: Transitives and Intransitives." Some students are quick to announce their knowledge on the subject. Others are clearly dismayed by the terminology. I move to the next slide: "Noun + Verb: The Intransitive Verb Pattern. *Katherine laughed.*" I read it aloud as they copy it down, accenting and alternating the words with their coinciding slots. "Noun (Katherine) + Verb (Laughed). Before I advance to the next slide, does anyone notice anything about the verb in this pattern?" Doug is quick to raise his hand.

"Well, the sentence is really short. There's not much to it."

"That's true, Doug, but it doesn't need anything else does it, Emily?"

She likes the simplicity of my question, responding, "No. It's a complete sentence. But you can add more, right?"

"Yes, you can. But you don't have to, because *laughed* is an intransitive verb. An intransitive verb is a verb that allows for completeness, needing no other words, other than a noun, in the sentence." I've clicked on the next slide; it contains the information I've just related, and the students are quick to copy it down. They seem to enjoy this easily digestible, but important, information. I continue to advance the slide show that illustrates the concept through graphic slots (sentence diagrams). The words *Katherine* and *laughed* zoom into their respective spots.

After reading the slide a few times, the students have grasped the concept. I move on. The next slide reads, "The queen laughed." The diagram is already there. Keith, always armed with a question, asks, "Why is the word *the* coming out of the word *queen*?" This is an easy one for me.

"*The* modifies *queen*, so it must have its own slot showing its relationship to *queen* in the sentence. Let's look at some other options for this pattern." The next slide reads, "Five purple circus elephants laughed." There is laughter in the room. Who says grammar isn't fun?

"As you can see, we can add adjectives to the noun *elephants*, but the slots are the same. The subject and verb are still in the pattern (*elephants laughed*); because the verb is intransitive, it requires nothing else." As they copy it down, I continue to click. Other options for verb endings fly into view. First, *Laughs*, followed by *laughs*, *is laughing*, *has laughed*, *was laughing*, and finally, *will laugh*. Again, the students' enthusiasm is apparent. Monica asks, "So you can change the tense and it's still an intransitive?"

"Sure is," I reply, bringing up the final slide for this pattern. Added to the verb endings is the prepositional phrase *at the movies*. I get more questions about the slots.

"Why is *movies* coming out of the *at* slot?"

And "Why is *the* attached to *movies*?"

Again, I explain that these words modify the words to which they are attached. I didn't see this question coming, but it proves a valuable way to explain each word's relationship to others in the sentence. To conclude this pattern, I ask the students to write their own sentences in the intransitive verb pattern, using characters from *The Scarlet Letter*.

Turning the music back on, I circle the room as students write, looking for responses that show quality understanding. After a few minutes, I call on specific students. "Okay, John, let's hear your sentence."

"Hester sinned."

"Nice job, John. You nailed it. *Sinned* is an intransitive verb, so it fits the pattern perfectly. How about your sentence, Michelle?"

"Chillingworth plotted."

"That's great, Michelle. Nice verb choice; it's very clear and appropriate. Now, does anyone have a more complex example?" Dan's hand is up. I've seen his sentence; it's a fine example.

"The minister, Dimmesdale, cried in secret."

I write the sentence on the board. "Wow, Dan! You even put in an appositive." I'm almost too eager to add in previously covered concepts. Amanda is quick to point this out.

"Mr. Oliva, you love those things."

"I do, Amanda. Do you know why? Because they add specific information that makes your writing more vivid! Let's diagram Dan's sentence together on the board." I hadn't planned this, but I can't resist the opportunity. We label the parts and put each word into its appropriate slot. The students have a chance to see the difficult branches created firsthand. It's time to move on.

The next slide introduces the transitive verb pattern. It reads, "Transitive Verb Pattern = Noun + Verb + Noun." The students copy this down, unsure of how it will look in sentence form. PowerPoint allows me to bring the lines in one at a time, to show the slots. "Everybody (noun) loves (transitive verb) Raymond (noun/direct object)." There's some impatience in the room. Jordan calls out, "What's a direct object?" I'm quick to say, "Don't worry, Jordan; I'm sure the next slide will clarify the term." And it does. It reads, "Transitive verbs take direct objects. Direct objects answer "who" or "what" about the action verbs." I sense some confusion about the transitive verb concept, so together we make a quick list for their notebooks.

"Let's think of some more transitive verbs. Remember: Transitive verbs do not stand alone. They require additional information in order to be complete."

"I've got one!" Lauren shouts out.

"Okay, let's have it, Lauren."

"*Finds.*"

"Good choice, Lauren. Any others?" Suddenly transitive verbs fly around the room.

"*Hates!*"

"*Believes!*"

After about twenty are quickly collected, I calm down the room and continue with the lesson. This concept is digested more rapidly because we've already covered the basics in the previous segment. I ask the students to write their own sentences using this pattern and their knowledge of the novel. They write for a few minutes and I survey their creations.

"The townspeople ostracize Hester."

"Pearl creates her own scarlet letter."

"Governor Bellingham tests Pearl."

Some students have trouble with this pattern, but the suggestions of their peers help clarify the concept for them. We discuss their sentences thoroughly, looking closely at any additional parts of speech added. I'm feeling confident in the lesson, even more so in my growth as a teacher of grammar.

With the period winding down, I'm hurrying a little, trying to fit in the two final patterns. The next slide reads, "Complex transitive verbs take indirect objects as well as direct objects. Indirect objects answer 'to whom,' 'for whom,' 'to what,' or 'for what' about the direct object." Now the students are collectively confused. Before they have a chance to voice their agitation, I say, "I know this is a lot of new information. Stick with me; the slides that follow will help illustrate this concept. You write sentences in this pattern all the time."

The students trust me. They copy the next slide diagram into their notebooks: "Noun + Verb + Noun + Noun." Now familiar, the slots zip in: "He/gave/gift/me," followed by "He gave me an unexpected gift." Together, we discuss the sentence by asking it questions.

"Who, or what, did he give?"

Cassie responds proudly, "A gift!"

"To whom did he give it, Shira?"

"To me!"

With each part labeled and the role of each word in the sentence analyzed, I ask the students to write their own sentences. They write and respond faster; their confidence equals mine. I'm in such a flurry to finish the lesson, so excited by our collective progress, that I fail to see the questions headed my way. The students' sentences are more complex now, and so are their questions.

"The town gave Hester a burden."

"Chillingworth told Hester a secret."

"Hester made Pearl a dress."

Christine, eager to satiate her curiosity, raises her hand first. "Mr. O., is it still called an indirect object if you switch the order of the words around?" Uh oh; I'm in trouble now.

Alissa has a similar concern. "Yeah, my sentence seems to fit, but the order is different."

You can really feel these moments coming on; an unexpected question equals instant sweat and a desire to crawl into a hole. I have no choice but to persevere and explore the question through honesty.

"Well, I'm not sure, Christine. Let's hear your sentence and see if we can figure this out."

She offers, "Hester made a dress for Pearl."

I'm stuck. Suddenly I can't think of even my most basic grammatical knowledge. With time running out and a few slides left, I try to break down the pattern, but get nowhere.

"In the pattern we've been working with, the sentence would read: *Hester made Pearl a dress*. It seems you've added a prepositional phrase, altering the pattern. To be honest, Christine, I'm not sure what you've got there. I'll have to check my sources and get back to you tomorrow. In fact, if you're dying to know, stop back after school; I'll have an answer by then."

I have to admit: It's not easy admitting what you don't know in front of a class. But students aren't as cynical as you might think. If handled correctly, sudden problems like this barely slow you down.

Swiftly, I reach the climax of the lesson. The slide rockets into view, alarming the class with its apparent complexity. I say, allaying their concern, "Remember when we started *The Scarlet Letter*? The language looked nearly impossible to decipher. But in time, with practice, perseverance, and a few reading techniques, you learned to read it with relative ease. This concept is no different. Give the information a chance to sink in." In their notebooks they write, "Patterns with Object Complements: A few verbs take object complements. Object complements are nouns, or noun phrases, that add information about the direct object." The next slide offers two examples. "The kids call their teacher Mrs. K." And "They consider Mrs. K. a pain in the neck." The slots help the students (and me!) realize how the object complements fit into the sentence. The following slide gives us a chance to test our skill. It reads, "The students consider the topic _____." We fill in the object complement slot on our own before advancing the show.

"Matt, how do you feel about the topic of the social repercussions associated with outsourcing business to developing countries?"

"Uh? Oh, I think I find it amazing, Mr. O. Truly fascinating." He replies with his best dry wit.

"Julien, what do you think about the topic of grammar?"

"I think it's interesting."

And I believe him. We're all learning, and this information seems really useful. The students recognize the role of the object complement, really just a modifier for the direct object, and it's time to write their own sentences.

I ask the students to complete the final piece of the lesson for homework, allowing them to have a little fun at my expense.

"For homework, write your own sentences employing the object complement. You may write your sentences about me—I'm sure there are a few opinions going around. But be careful. Don't be disrespectful; just have a little friendly fun. Make sure you clearly identify the object complement. Great effort today! See you tomorrow with those sentences!"

Whew! What a lesson! Although the content appeared simple, there are often unexpected questions when teaching a grammatical concept for the first time. But what you don't know, you learn, and before long, you're the expert others seek out in a bind.

In case you were wondering, here's the answer to Christine's question: Both versions mean the same thing, obviously: ". . . for Pearl" is an indirect object in the form of a prepositional phrase. The English language allows for a choice: You can use the indirect object pattern, in which you insert the receiver of the direct object between the verb and the direct object, or you can get the same message across by shifting the indirect object to the end of the sentence, in the form of a prepositional phrase.

Here is another example, this time from Alissa:

Hester gives her hand-knitted gloves <u>to the governor</u>.

Now, if you were to use a pronoun to replace the direct object, *her hand-knitted gloves*, you'd have to shift the indirect object to the end and say it as a prepositional phrase. You would never say: *Hester gives the governor them*. And you certainly would not say: *Hester gives him them*. You'd say: *Hester gives them to the governor*, or *Hester gives them to him*.

This is the end of what I'm calling Part I, foundational information about the basics of grammar that all speakers of the English language know unconsciously. Part II shows you how to bring what you know about grammar to your students in actual classroom practice.

II Classroom Practice

4 Natural Expertise about Grammar

The purpose of this chapter is to get you started on your new kind of grammar instruction. This is instruction that will capitalize on students' vast unconscious knowledge of grammar and will use that knowledge as a foundation for the organized information you want them to know.

Students come to us with astonishing expertise about language. In that sense, we *don't have to* teach them grammar! They already know it: They know how an English sentence is formed; they know that the roles of the subject and the object are signified by the placement of those words relative to the verb, and they can even recognize an inversion; they know how to line up adjectives and other modifiers in order and, again, they can recognize an inversion when they see adjectives in the post-noun position. They know how to conjugate verbs according to rules and according to the idiosyncratic patterns of the many irregular verbs in the English language. They know how to use pronouns as stand-ins for noun phrases. They know how to flip words into service as different parts of speech, and they know how to add endings to shift and adapt words into other forms: nouns, verbs, adjectives, adverbs. This is just a smattering of our students' remarkable ability to learn language and make it do their will in accordance with rules, rules that we can't necessarily articulate but that are nevertheless there, in the hardwiring of our brains. When we teach grammar, we are helping students to think about and recognize and use their subconscious grammar knowledge in a conscious way.

I suggest we begin our exploration of language, our study of grammar, with something that everyone loves: nonsense language. It is through nonsense language that we can reveal to students, to their delight, how much they actually know about grammar. I'll give you two examples here. At the close of this chapter in his Teacher's Journal, Tom explains a well-developed classroom experience.

At any grade level, you can begin with the first stanza of "Jabberwocky":

"T'was brillig, and the slithy toves
Did gyre and gimble in the wabe.
All mimsy was the borogrove,
And the mome raths outgrabe.

Engage students in a conversation about the meaning of this stanza. They will of course know that it was a brillig day, a day on which some toves, slithy ones, were gyring and gimbling in something called a wabe. Obviously, a wabe would be a place. We don't know much about this place (as there are no adjectives to describe it further) except that gyring and gimbling apparently go on there. We don't know much about what toves are, but we do know that there are more than one of them. We know that the toves gyred and gimbled at some finite point in the past. We have two cues for this time zone: *T'was* and *did*.

From the second sentence, we know that the borogrove was mimsy. This is interesting because this sentence is presented as a reversal of the usual spoken English pattern. However, not only will students recognize it as a meaningful English sentence, but they will also recognize the reversal as a pattern often found in poetry. "It just sounds like poetry or a story" they will say. They will know that "The borogrove was all mimsy" is another way to say the exact same thing. The borogrove was all mimsy and the raths were outgrabe. *Outgrabe* is puzzling: At first, it does sound like a verb; however, it's probably not a verb because if it were it would have a past-tense ending. It is more likely an adjective that is used poetically in the post-noun position. So we have a mimsy borogrove and outgrabe raths on this brillig day. What kind of raths? Mome ones. You could even speculate the fact that the condition of momeness is more intrinsic to raths than that of being outgrabe, but this is a fine point.

(Notice that as we explicate meaning in the nonsense language, we ignore any qualitative meaning that may be evoked by similarities between the nonsense words and real words, such as the fact that "slithy" may remind us of "slithering" or "slimy" or that "toves" may remind us of "toads." We extract meaning entirely from grammatical cues. It is this ability to extract meaning from word relationships and word formations alone that justifies the value of this activity as a grammar lesson.)

As you speak of the language in "Jabberwocky," use grammatical language incidentally and naturally. If your students are in the upper elementary grades or above, they have heard of nouns, verbs, adjectives, adverbs, prepositions, tenses, and maybe other grammatical terms, but they have probably never actually used these terms to discuss meaning. They have probably used these terms only in very clinical settings, such as to do exercises in the grammar book in which they pick out certain parts of speech. Your use of these terms in a natural context to talk about language—your modeling—will convey the convenience of having such terms available.

Extending the lesson, you can present more nonsense language:

> I found a fleek.
> I found a frippish fleek.
> The fleek that I found was frippish.
> The fleek frippishly flindered.
> I found a flindering fleek on the floot.

You can ask a series of questions, using grammatical terminology: How do you know that *fleek* is a noun? If you had more than one *fleek*, what would you call it? What if a *floot* had the qualities of a *fleek*? How would you describe the *floot*? How do you know that *frippish* is an adjective? When did the *fleek flinder*? How do you know that *flinder* is a verb? How else can you use the word *flinder* in a sentence that indicates that *flinder* is an action?

What have we accomplished with this exploration of nonsense language? Is what we have accomplished worthwhile? How do we know that we've accomplished something worthwhile? I like to plan and reflect using the Understanding by Design (UBD) paradigm developed by Grant Wiggins and Jay McTighe. In this model, we begin by deciding what concepts, understandings, and skills we want students to attain as a result of a learning experience. Then we consider what would be acceptable evidence of learning (assessment). Then we settle on the content: What materials and activities would best deliver us to our intended destination? A UBD map would look like the one in Figure 4.1.

The value of UBD is that it sets the teacher's sights beyond specific content. Rather than saying, "I'm teaching adjectives," the teacher is thinking, "I'm teaching how sentences are enriched and clarified by various grammatical structures and how they are placed within the sentence. When students can write sentences that deploy adjective structures effectively, and when they can use the proper terminology to describe what they've done, then I'll have acceptable evidence of learning. I'll use literary text, model sentences, and student-generated sentences as the vehicle for teaching this."

Teaching Grammar with the Brain in Mind

Research in brain-compatible learning supports teaching through patterns (Jensen 48). The human brain understands the world through patterns: The brain is a pattern-seeking device. Because grammar hap-

Concepts, Understandings, Skills: *What do I want students to learn?*	Acceptable Evidence of Learning: *How will I know what they've learned?*	Content, Activities: *How will I engage them in a meaningful learning experience?*
I want students to learn that they already have the natural ability to discern parts of speech because they have a sense of the patterns of English grammar. I want students to understand how words adapt themselves into different parts of speech. I want students to know that grammar is pattern based. I want students to use frames and forms to identify nouns and verbs: Noun: Can be preceded by *the*; can be made possessive Verb: Can be preceded by an auxiliary (form of *have* or *be*); can have an *-ing* form; can be negated in the sentence Adjective: Can be preceded by *very*; can fit into this frame: *The_____truck is very_____*; is often formed from a noun or a verb with an ending such as *-er, -y, -ish, -ous, -al, -able*, and others Adverb: Answers these questions: When? Where? How? Why? In what manner?; often has *-ly* ending; *-ly* adverbs can be preceded by *very*	Students already know how to form English sentences. They will reveal that they understand the patterned nature of English sentences when they can: 1. Generate questions about word relationships and sentence meanings in sentences that have nonsense words. 2. Generate original sentences using nonsense words. Their nonsense words must look and sound like English words. 3. Draw models of English sentences, using blank spaces to indicate an understanding of grammatical patterns.	I will give students the first stanza of "Jabberwocky" and other nonsense sentences. Students will answer questions that will lead them to discover their ability to understand how a word's form and position give important meaning cues. They will modify the nonsense words, adapting them to other grammatical functions.

Figure 4.1. Planning guide.

pens to be a pattern-generating system, the brain and grammar instruction that is based on patterns should get along just fine.

I'd like to connect effective grammar instruction even more specifically to the work of Eric Jensen. According to Jensen, learning experiences that are most likely to be durable and meaningful are those that are sociable, pattern based, sensory, emotionally nonthreatening, energetic, choice based, relevant to the student's own world, and meaning based. Conversely, the human brain is least disposed to learning when the contents and processes are 100 percent decided by someone else (when students are offered no choices), when the contents are perceived as irrelevant and disconnected from the real world (e.g., when learning is seen as being only for a test), and when the learner experiences negative emotions (e.g., fear, anger, confusion, boredom).

In keeping with brain-compatible pedagogy, I suggest that you incorporate the following elements into grammar instruction. *The Cambridge Encyclopedia of the English Language* by David Crystal is a treasure trove of activities, some of which are suggested below.

1. Socialization: Make learning grammar a sociable experience. Invite students to freely contribute their own language, especially if that means they bring dialect and slang. Dialect and slang are perfect teachable moments to show that language changes, language varies, language is rule-governed, and language characterizes the speaker as a member or nonmember of a speech community.

   a. Language changes: Words themselves go in and out of style. Nouns that name things no longer used, such as a *bodkin*, fall into disuse. New things come along that need to be named. Pronunciation, syntax, even graphology changes over time. Understanding that language is a fluid social contract is essential before meaningful, informed grammar instruction can begin. Get students to think of language as belonging to a set of social contracts that includes dress, manners, forms of greeting and leave-taking. If you want to spark a lively discussion, ask students to name expressions that their parents and grandparents use that would not be used by their own generation.

   b. Language varies: Everyone is interested in regional dialects as well as the differences between them. Solicit from students various ways of saying and pronouncing certain words in different parts of the country.

   c. Language is rule-governed: The biggest excuse for language prejudice is the fallacy that dialects other than Standard English are not rule-governed. See www.askoxford.com/worldofwords/history/?view=uk.

2. Humor: Fortunately, language and humor make a friendly pair. Nonsense words, made-up words, different ways of saying things, word games, rhythm and rhyme—these are some of the natural ways to connect language to the funny bone.

3. Metaphor: Metaphors allow the learner to link new concepts to familiar ones, thereby making comfortable space for new knowledge to fit into the brain. But metaphors also shape how we regard things. Negative metaphors can poison the new knowledge, so we have to be careful to make our metaphors positive and even playful.

The power of using metaphor as a teaching tool and understanding how the metaphors all around us work to shape our thinking is explored in two books published by NCTE: *Bridging: A Teacher's Guide to Metaphorical Thinking* and *Metaphorical Ways of Knowing: The Imaginative Nature of Thought and Expression*. Both books are by Sharon L. Pugh and colleagues. In the epigraph to Part I of the latter book, the authors quote Howard A. Peelle (author of *Computer Metaphors*): "Metaphors offer a ready perspective for comprehending something new. They are particularly useful at an early stage of learning: They provide a starting place; they make connections to that which is already well-understood; they suggest possibilities for further exploration" (11).

To teach the concept of adjectives and adjectivals, we can use a cooking metaphor: Adjectives (and adjectivals) are the **spice** of the dish. Like spices, they lend distinctive flavor when used judiciously and artfully. But, like spices, adjectives are not the substance of the dish. And adjectives can be overadded, revealing the injudiciousness, and not the skill, of the chef.

To teach the concept of coordinating conjunctions, we can use the metaphor of links in a chain. Conjunctions link grammatical structures together. In so doing, they set up relationships between the sides being linked. The most common connections are *and* (establishing equality), *but* (establishing contrast), *or/nor* (establishing choice), and *so* (establishing cause and effect). Just as a chain can link light things or heavy things, coordinating conjunctions can be strong enough to link clauses (heavy) or light enough to link phrases or single words. Heavy links—those that link clauses—need the fortification of a comma to make them strong enough.

To teach the concept of the sentence patterns, we can use the metaphor of a neighborhood. In most neighborhoods, the houses look different—have different layouts, different entrance foyers, varying numbers of rooms. Some have rooms all on one level; others have multilevels with stairs between. But they all divide their space into rooms;

all have similar kinds of rooms in common; and all are built for the same purpose: to provide housing for people. When you enter a house whose pattern you know, you don't have to think too much about your movements within that house. You have a sense of familiarity that enables you to concentrate on other matters while in that house, not on how to find your way to the room that will serve your immediate purpose. Likewise, sentences form patterns. Sentences can be stark or elaborate, but all have basic elements that fall into certain expected places lest we get lost within them. So the "house on the block" metaphor works to illustrate how pattern-finding, in language as in houses, helps us make sense of the world.

Another metaphor for the sentence patterns is a menu. A menu is a list of choices divided into courses. What you select as your appetizer, your beverage, your entrée, and your dessert are all supposed to blend together pleasantly. Each choice will affect others: You wouldn't order eggplant rolatini as an appetizer and then eggplant parmesan for your entrée, would you? Similarly, sentences fall into "courses" called "slots." What you select for your subject slot must agree with what you select as your verb.

To teach the concept of the semicolon as a way to separate closely related independent clauses, I like to use the bride and groom as a metaphor. Semicolons are but one of the ways in which two clauses that are similar in meaning and in structure can get hitched. (*Sometimes you feel like a nut; sometimes you don't.*) Just as a couple can get married by a member of the clergy or by a civil figure of authority, so two independent clauses can be unified by a semicolon, if they so choose, or by a comma along with a coordinating conjunction.

The common error is to find only one member of the wedding party present and whole. Independent Clause the First walks down the aisle and waits at the altar for Independent Clause the Second. Imagine his or her chagrin when only *part* of Clause the Second appears. When a semicolon is clearly in place to unify two grammatical elements, we do expect an independent clause to follow that semicolon, just as we expect two complete humans to show up at their own wedding.

To teach the concept of the independent clause, I borrow a metaphor from Pamela Dykstra's *Rhythms of Writing*. An independent clause (sentence) is like a bicycle, not a unicycle. You can have all kinds of bells, whistles, lights, and reflectors on it, but a bicycle has got to have two wheels that work together. An independent clause, similarly, must have two parts—a subject and a predicate—that work together. Just as a wheel has a hub, a subject must have a noun; a predicate must have a verb.

To teach the concept of the dependent (subordinate) clause, I use the wagon metaphor. This wagon is like a dependent clause: It can do work, but it needs to be hitched to something bigger than itself. It can't propel itself; it must be led by another wheeled structure. And, of course, there are different kinds of hitches (conjunctions).

Parallel structure is hard to understand in concept but easy to recognize through example. To teach what parallel structure is, I use the metaphor of a chorus. Choral singing shows an organization, a sense of common purpose achieved through uniformity of appearance and action, that links to parallel structure. This metaphor is particularly apt because parallel structure creates musicality in discourse.

And finally, I borrow a metaphor from Cornelia Paraskevas, professor of linguistics at Western Oregon University. When she took up the hobby of quilting, Cornelia noticed how quilting is similar to grammar. Both work within patterns that can express infinite variety. The quilter creates units that consist of compound parts, increasingly added to and used as a unit to create bigger units. The "language quilt" consists of kinds of words (parts of speech) that attach to other parts to form phrases, then to form clauses, then sentences, then paragraphs, and finally the wholeness of text.

Dividing Sentences into Parts

When we learn grammar, we divide sentences into discrete parts and we name the parts. Sentences divide into clauses. Clauses divide into phrases. Phrases divide into words. Clauses, phrases, words—these are the components of syntax. Fortunately, students come to us with a reliable sense of where sentences divide into subjects and predicates. We need to start our grammar instruction revealing to them that they have that innate sense of sentence division. How are you going to go about doing this?

Mrs. Callari and Mrs. Lehrer both teach eighth grade. Mrs. Callari uses a traditional grammar book. Mrs. Lehrer uses visuals, manipulatives, and literature to teach grammar. Mrs. Callari begins this year's grammar instruction by saying: "I know that you've learned about subjects and predicates. Do the exercise on page 15. The directions tell you to underline the subjects once and the predicates twice." Mrs. Callari's students are thinking (and saying): "This again? Why do we have to do this in English every year?"

Mrs. Lehrer begins her grammar instruction by giving students manipulatives that she has fashioned out of small plastic interlocking cubes, each about one inch long. Each panel on the cubes has a word.

Mrs. Lehrer has color-coded the cubes with markers. Nouns are green; verbs are yellow; adjectives are red; prepositions are blue; pronouns are light green; conjunctions are purple; adverbs are orange; determiners are turquoise; auxiliaries are gold. As students settle in, Mrs. Lehrer scoops up handfuls of cubes and puts them on students' (adjoining) desks. Immediately, and with no instruction, students busily link the cubes to form sentences: *He sang a very big pizza. My fish had ten beautiful kittens. I hate a little rain.* There are smiles all around as the students grab cubes from one anothers' collections to lengthen their sentences. Spontaneously, a competition develops as to who can concoct the longest, most preposterous sentence. But preposterous in meaning as the sentences may be, *all of them are grammatically correct!* Repeat: Without knowing that this is a grammar lesson, not a single student does not know that he or she is supposed to create a sentence that make sense in accordance with the rules of English grammar, and that is what they all do. Every single one of them.

When everybody has a sentence, Mrs. Lehrer calls on a few students to come to the front of the room to show their sentences. She instructs them to hold their sentences in two hands so that the class can read them. She then says, "OK, now divide your sentence into two parts. Hold each part in one hand. Move your hands apart so we can see the two parts of the sentence." When that is done, she has the class members who are at their seats do the same. She checks to make sure everyone's sentences are divided into subject and predicate components. She then tells them, "OK, now take the part that is in your right hand and pass it to the person on your right." They do so, and discover that they still have grammatically intact sentences (although some are now without subject-verb agreement). It is at this point that Mrs. Lehrer introduces the grammatical terminology of subject and predicate: "Who remembers what the two parts of the sentence are called?" She has no trouble getting the students to recognize subjects and predicates.

Mrs. Callari. Mrs. Lehrer. The first presides over a dreary, factory-model exercise, working with language the students don't care about. They've done this before and they don't see why they are doing it again. But Mrs. Lehrer's students are excited about learning about language. They use their own hands and voices to create sentences that delight them because of their impossibility—and yet possibility.

You can easily make your own set of "grammar cubes." Get a set of LEGOs, cover them with adhesive labels, and use colorful markers to write words on them. LEGOs don't come in the variety of colors that correspond to the parts of speech you will need. They come in white, green, purple, blue, yellow, and red. You can cover some of the white ones with adhesive labels of another color to complete this set of speech parts. One more modification: LEGOs don't link together horizontally, as words in a sentence need to do, so you'll need to affix small, button-sized Velcro circles on the sides of each block.

Flash Cards

Ordinarily, I'm not a fan of flash cards because I think of them as being used only for drill. However, I've used flash cards—I call them "noun cards"—in the early stages of my grammar instruction to show students the flexibility of the English language.

Let's say I have a box of flash cards—the kind that are used to teach young children "sight words"—with pictures of animals and other familiar objects on them. These are my noun cards. The first thing I do is establish the "The _____" frame. I give each student a flash card and say, "These are noun cards. Does anyone have a picture of something you can't put the word *the* in front of?" The students smile and look at one another. No hands go up. "Let's make a rule," I say. "If you can put the word *the* in front of a word, then that word is a noun." (But what if an adjective intervenes between *the* and the noun? I need to clarify by asking for a single word, not a phrase, that tells what is on the card.) I go on to say: "Tell me, in a phrase that has one word with *the* in front of it, what is on your card." They tell me: *The cake. The rabbit. The hat.* I say, "Is there anyone who can't turn their noun into a possessive by adding apostrophe *s* and then another noun to show ownership?" There's some confusion. "OK, let's take the word *book*. Put an apostrophe *s* after your noun and then put the word *book* after it. Is there anyone who can't do that?" Now they get it. *The cake's book. The rabbit's book.* "Let's make a rule: A noun is a word that you can make possessive by adding apostrophe *s*."

From there, we establish the concept of a functional shift. It's easy for students to see that the noun *duck* does adjective work when we say "duck pond." In turn, *pond* can modify the noun *water*. This goes to show that not just adjectives can answer the question "what kind?" about a noun. When a word that is a noun in form (*duck*) answers the "what kind?" question, that noun is functioning *adjectivally*. We say that it is a noun in form but an adjectival in function.

Tag ("Stick-on") Questions

Students vex us by writing unintentional sentence fragments. We've told them (again and again) that "a sentence expresses a complete thought," but this explanation doesn't seem to work as well as it should.

A tag question, also called a mini-question or even a "stick-on" question, is a little question of verification, tagged on to the end of a positive or negative declarative sentence, used to confirm the truth of the declaration. Only *declarative* sentences come into play when we are talking about sentence fragments. (Writers don't commit "question fragments" or "command fragments" or "exclamation fragments.") A declarative sentence accepts a tag question, like this:

> You don't live in New Jersey, *do you?*
>
> Emma lives in Nutley Park, *doesn't she?*
>
> You can take the King's Crossing bridge, *can't you?*
>
> I'm not the best person to ask for directions, *am I?*

Here are some familiar sentence fragments which, you'll notice, do not accept a tag question for verification:

> *Where I live.
>
> *When Emily moved to Nutley Park.
>
> *Because I found a dollar in the street.

Note that, at first, students may think they can add a tag question (*Because I found a dollar in the street, didn't I?*). With a little prodding, however, they will see that something is missing: The tag question doesn't take the *entire* sentence (fragment) into account. It doesn't include the first word of the fragment, and that's because this first word is causing the group of words to be a fragment.

Native speakers of English can form such questions automatically; English language learners have a lot to learn to achieve this skill. The value of the tag question is that *you can't make one if the "sentence" is not a sentence*. Thus, the tag question technique is a handy way to check for sentence completeness. Granted, it works only for declarative sentences, but declarative sentences are the only class of sentences that gives us trouble as far as sentence completeness goes.

Other similar test frames for sentence completeness are the yes/no question and the "It is true that . . ." frame. The former posits that if you can turn a statement into a yes/no question, then it is a complete sentence. (*Does Emma live in Nutley Park? Can you take the King's Crossing bridge?*). The latter posits that if you can precede a group of words with "It is true that . . . ," then that group of words is in fact a complete

---

*The asterisk is the symbol that linguists use to signify grammatical incorrectness that serves the purpose of illustrating a point.

sentence. These tests for sentence completeness are developed in detail by Rei Noguchi in his *Grammar and the Teaching of Writing: Limits and Possibilities*.

To make this method of testing for sentence completeness visual and manipulative, I like to use actual tags. Using sticky notes, you can have students go up to a display board on which text has been written. Have the students literally stick a tag question onto each group of words purporting to be a sentence. In the majority of cases, unintentional sentence fragments are subordinate clauses that are attempting to strike out on their own. Most of the time, the remedy is to attach the unintentional sentence fragment (subordinate clause) to the previous sentence.

Conclusion

At this point in your grammar teaching, by using nonsense language, tag questions, visuals, and manipulatives, you will have accomplished the following:

1. Students are excited about learning grammar because they know it is accessible to them and that they can use the vast amount they already know to learn more.

2. Students have learned not only that a clause has two parts—a subject and a predicate—but that if they write with awareness of these two parts, they can produce more interesting sentences. They can expand or contract the subject and/or the predicate. They can enliven their sentences by placing people in the subject slots and by employing action verbs.

3. Students have learned how to edit for sentence completeness.

TEACHER'S JOURNAL

My students come to class expecting an introductory lesson for the Nathaniel Hawthorne novel *The Scarlet Letter*. What they don't know is that the novel, a challenging read full of complex syntax and ornate vocabulary, is the perfect launching pad for discussing word order in a sentence and for contemplating how word order can help inform their reading. The goal of this lesson is to show students that they understand language through grammar. To do this, we'll use an activity inspired by Craig Hancock in his *Meaning-Centered Grammar* (18).

It's a rainy November day. I'm playing "Gone" by the Beta Band as students enter, creating a focused atmosphere for learning. As they settle in, I ask them to turn to the grammar section of their notebooks. The groaning is subdued; they know that our grammar studies are often more exciting than the average lesson.

Their attention is on the board where I've written:

Stiggy

His

The

The

With

Mished

Trambulator

Floop

Glorch

With the tunes pulsing in the background, I explain the goal of the lesson: to illuminate what they already know about grammar and how such knowledge helps them understand language. Excited about harnessing the moment, I say, "You know who, or what, the agent of the sentence is, the action and tense, the receiver of the action, and the instrument of the action. And you know all of these things even when you don't know what the words mean. Now I'm going to prove this to you, and we're going to do it with words you may have never heard. We might even squeeze in some difficult phrases from *The Scarlet Letter*."

I ask the students to write a sentence using the words written on the board. They look confused. I explain that they should use all the words, in their original form. "Just try to write a sentence that makes sense. Be creative; you don't have to know what they mean!" I turn up the tunes, building the mood. At first they're quiet; most don't know what to think, what to write. Ironically, I don't know exactly what to expect either. I watch them twirl their pens and bite their lips, and then the hands go up.

"Do I have to use the second *the*?" Zach asks.

Amy wonders in her best teen lingo, "Can we, like, use commas?"

Shira asks for everyone, "Do we have to use all the words?"

"Yes," I repeat calmly, "Use all the words in the list, and only those words."

Juliet, with a restless readiness, chimes in, "How about hyphens. . . . Can we use hyphens?"

Turning up the music to mark this as a final comment imploring them to dig down and get it done, I add, "Yes! Hyphen away! Feel free to use any punctuation you wish. Just write a sentence that employs all the words in the list in their original form."

Now they're writing. I circle the room looking in on their creations, adding approval or suggestions. I announce, "One minute!" Josh and Stephen are already sharing. Lindsey and Danny are too.

Circling, I turn off the music and ask Marni, an outgoing, imaginative student, if she has a "stiggy floop."

"Oh yeah," she replies. "I have a couple."

I shout across the room, "Hey Tim, how often do you mish?" With this spontaneity, I realize immediately the importance of making this a casual conversation. It shouldn't feel like work.

Lisa yells out, "Oh! I've got it!" And I know it's time to regroup.

To attract their attention, I say, "I'd like to hear a few of your sentences, and I want you to think about the word order, where each word is placed in your sentence." I move over to the board and circle *stiggy*, *mished*, *trambulator*, *floop*, and *glorch*. With increased emphasis, I say, "I have a confession to make. These words don't exist. I made them up! But because of where you put them in your sentence, they make sense, don't they? You've already established what you know about grammar." I add, to comfort those who are having trouble with the activity, "If your sentence doesn't seem to make sense, it may be because you don't see that you can have a stiggy trambulator. Or that there is only one option for a verb in your sentence: the word *mished*." They're calling out now, but I don't mind.

Corey and Brandon, twins, shout out, "I got mished!"

The activity is in full swing. Kristen offers her sentence first. She's feeling smart and inventive when she proclaims, "The stiggy glorch mished his floop with the trambulator." I'm quick to tell her that it's better than mine.

I ask the class collectively, "What kind of glorch?"

And nearly all of them call out, "Stiggy!" I ask for another sentence.

Lindsey states seriously, "Stiggy, the floop, mished the glorch with his trambulator."

I'm adding a humorous tone to the responses, simultaneously uncovering the concepts of the lesson: "The trambulator. That's a serious instrument." And, "I'm a big misher."

We gather a series of sentences. It's a nice way to give every student a chance to be heard. Nearly everyone nails it pretty quickly. Alexa announces that she wrote an appositive. Now I'm excited. We're applying skills illuminated in other lessons. This grammar stuff is sinking in and adding depth to their writing. I ask Alexa what the details in her appositive are doing.

"They give information about the trambulator," she says with confidence.

I add, "Alexa, you know a lot about grammar. You know that with the appositive you're renaming, or clarifying, the agent, or subject, of your sentence."

I select a few of their sentences and write them on the board. Then I ask the students to write them in their notebooks so we can analyze what we've already accomplished together.

"Erica, can you tell me—take a wild stab out of thin air—what the agent of this sentence is?"

Without hesitation she replies, "The glorch."

"That's right," I say, adding, "What's another word for the agent, Erica?"

"The subject."

"So you know that the subject of this sentence is the glorch, even though you have no idea what a glorch is; how do you know that, Erica?"

Almost annoyed, she responds, "Because of where it is!"

We're on a roll!

"Alexa, can you tell me what the action of this sentence is?"

"Mished!"

Building steam, I ask, "Now Alexa, I'm pretty sure you've never mished. How did you know that mished was the verb of this sentence?"

Politely, and a little unsure, she replies, "Well, a lot of verbs end in -*ed*."

"And what does that -*ed* tell us about the action of this sentence, Alexa?" I can see her swell with the strength of her knowledge.

"It tells us that the action happened in the past."

I need to make sure everyone is getting this, so I decide to clarify the concept of tense for the class. It's odd, but they seem to grasp the idea better because we're using words they've never seen. I say, "So the action is *mished*, and we know it is past tense because it's not *mishing*; it *mished*; it already happened."

This lesson is a blast to teach. Everyone is involved in creative and productive thought, analysis, and writing. And they seem to be internalizing the concepts with a precision I couldn't predict. Any surprises that emerge are easy to diffuse; this is a bomb I'm happy to see explode.

I'm eager to engage the next step of the activity when I ask, "What is the receiver, or direct object, of the sentence? What did the glorch mish?"

Suzi, quiet thus far, raises her hand. "The floop?"

"Yes, Suzi, the floop!" They're getting restless. This is almost too easy now; word order is slapping them in the face! I'm moving quickly when I add, "What is the instrument of the action?"

Andrew's hand is up, "It's the trambulator."

"That's right, Andrew. Oh, Brandon, what kind of trambulator is it?"

"It's a stiggy trambulator."

"What part of speech is a trambulator, Brandon?"

"It's a noun."

"And when a word comes before a noun and gives you information about that noun, especially when the word ends in *y*, what part of speech is that word?"

"It's an adjective."

I'm thrilled that the discussion of grammar is flowing so freely, progressing so naturally, and that my most reluctant learners are volunteering responses!

Keeping things upbeat and trying to strengthen their understanding of the concept, I write on the board:

Big

His

The

The

With

Hit

Umbrella

Man

Dog

Again, I ask students to compose a sentence using all of the words in the list. "I want you to use all of them and don't change them from their original form." This time there are no questions. I turn on the music and the room is silent. They are trying to impress, but I see that they are thinking too. Understanding word order has informed their writing. I make general comments: "Isn't it amazing when you know the words?"; "Consider how your knowledge of word order informs your sentence structure."

The students are eager to discuss their sentences as I circle the room. Knowing the words has made them bold; without realizing it, they have added layers of complexity to what they already know about grammar. To save time, I take a sentence from Esther and write it on the board: "The man hit the dog with his big umbrella." I get a few others verbally from the class and then look closer at Esther's.

"What words are movable in the sentence?"

Tim offers, "You can switch *man* with *dog*, even though it doesn't make as much sense."

Looking for further understanding, I ask, "Why can you move the word *dog* around in this sentence?"

Frank, shy but quite bright, finally gets involved, "You can move any of the nouns into the subject slot."

"That's right, Frank. Actually, you can move the nouns around quite a bit." I like his word choice: *slots*. We discuss the options for the sentence using this term, agreeing that the nouns, the preposition, and certainly the adjective *big* can all be moved pretty loosely. In fact, *big* can be attached to any noun because it's an adjective. After various suggestions and a lively discussion, I finish by offering one option I didn't hear: "Don't forget that you can add variety to your writing by employing a reversal; all you have to do is use a comma. For example, you can write: *With his umbrella, the man hit the big dog.*"

To wrap up the lesson, I use a sentence from *The Scarlet Letter*. On the board, I write: "I have striven with my young brother here" (63). I explain that even if they don't know what the word *striven* means, they can at least determine its purpose based on word order. The class period is winding down and I'm moving quickly.

I ask, "What have 'I' done?" In near unison, they reply, "Striven!"

"And when did 'I' do it?"

Again they respond together, "In the past!"

I'm beginning to think my lesson was a success. I explain that the word *striven* changes depending on where it's placed in the sentence. On the board, I write: *Would you like some striven with that?* I go around the room, hamming it up, offering invisible striven from an invisible pot.

"What part of speech is the verb *striven* here, Jenny?"

"It's a noun."

I make my way back to the board and write *I put on my striven hat*, mimicking the motion in pantomime.

"What kind of hat, Juliet?"

"A striven hat!"

And with that, we're out of time. With my final two minutes, I give a quick homework assignment previously prepared on a worksheet. I need to see if the students can show the same understanding independently with challenging material. The handout looks like this:

> This sentence is from the novel *The Scarlet Letter*. It contains a few words you probably don't know and exemplifies the complex, ornate language typical of Nathaniel Hawthorne, the author. <u>DO NOT LOOK THESE WORDS UP IN A DICTIONARY!</u> Using knowledge acquired in class today, identify the following in the sentence:
>
> - The Agent (the subject)

- The Action and Tense (the verb)
- The Receiver of the Action (the direct object)
- The Instrument of the Action (in this case = the object of the preposition)
- The Adjective(s)

Among any other population, or at a later period in the history of New England, the grim rigidity that petrified the bearded physiognomies of these good people would have augured some awful business in hand. (47)

In a few sentences, explain how your knowledge of word order helps you answer these questions.

This activity is challenging, but it will help generate a conversation essential to our reading of the text, as well as illuminate students' comprehension of the concepts covered in the lesson. The bell rings, and the strange words that spawned my lesson echo in my ears. Grammar is alive in my classroom, and I'm excited for my students.

5 Usage and Mechanics in Formal and Informal English

It's Thanksgiving. Opening the drawer to the sideboard in which you keep your fine china, you hear the slight clink of dish against dish as the heavily laden drawer rattles slightly on its track. Cautiously, you pull out case after case of dishes, saucers, and plates that have been encased in zippered, quilted covers to protect them from dust. You set the table on which your linen tablecloth has been draped and matching linen napkins skillfully folded. You set down your best glassware: water tumblers, wine goblets, champagne flutes. The silverware, newly polished and arranged in formal order, gleams at each setting. Everything is in place; the table sparkles invitingly.

It's Super Bowl Sunday. You pull out the large ceramic bowl with the Tex-Mex motif. You fill it to overflowing with those large triangular corn-based chips that will stand up to the guacamole and salsa that will fill the smaller bowls in the matching set. You set out a stack of small paper napkins and matching paper plates. You set half a dozen beer mugs into the freezer, awaiting your guests.

It's the Fourth of July. You grab the big metal serving tray, metal tongs, and long-handled spatula. You remove the hot dog buns and the burger buns from their plastic bags and stack them next to the grill. With a large serving spoon, you spoon out a couple of pounds of ready-made potato salad and coleslaw into plastic serving dishes. You throw some plastic forks, spoons, and knives into separate plastic tumblers and set them down on the plastic tablecloth that covers the glass picnic table on your deck. You roll open the table umbrella, protecting your guests from the sun.

Which of these customs is correct? Which are wrong? What would your guests think if you were to mix-and-match these dining styles, setting down silver-plated knives to cut the Fourth of July watermelon? Your guests might think you were a little weird.

Styles for hospitality, styles for clothing, styles for speech, styles for writing: These are social codes. They vary from group to group, from occasion to occasion. We learn them because we want to be accepted by a group. Most of our learning comes through watching others, but we may need to supplement that with "book learning" for the formal occasions, such as dining at the White House, that we have never actually experienced before. John Warriner, eponymous author of the widely used English grammar textbook series, is our Letitia Baldrige, famous Washington etiquette consultant.

As you type up the last touches on your master's thesis, you consult the official style guide required by your university. As you proofread a letter to your students' parents describing an upcoming field trip, you scan for lapses against Standard Written English rules, but you affect a friendly tone of diction and syntax so as to sound enthusiastic and hospitable. And as you contact your friends to round them up for a social event this weekend, you dash off an email, lavish with abbreviations.

You see the point. Communication styles vary in formality depending on the audience and purpose. To use the wrong register in a social milieu is to mark yourself as an outsider, a person who doesn't know the rules. Linguists use the term *code-switching* to refer to the practice of adjusting the level of formality of language to suit the situation.

How do we teach the difference between informal and formal usage in a way that is more engaging than having students do drill exercises out of a grammar book or read through handbooks of proper usage? The former fails because of lack of transfer from contrived language to authentic language; the latter fails because we don't learn the rules of language from a handbook any more than we learn the rules of a contact sport by reading about it. We learn as the game is afoot.

I am not a proponent of "grammar games" that are simply drill exercises in another form. Bingo games that match the name of a part of speech to its definition on a card do not impress me. Nor do the likes of races, card games, board games, or other gimmicks that keep students playing at low levels of "right" or "wrong" when it comes to their thinking about language. Worst of all, in my opinion, are those dreadful "gotcha"-type games that set students up as smug little pedants, gleefully (and obnoxiously) "correcting" one anothers' language. These "games" teach the wrong lesson about the nature of language and social interaction.

Usage is about context (audience and purpose). Effective language is language that is well suited to the context. The traditional way to "teach" usage (and it's usually ineffective) is this: The teacher gives a rule of Standard English, such as *Subjects and verbs must agree with each other in number*. The teacher then explains what this concept means, giving examples. Students then are given an exercise in which two verbs, one agreeing with the subject and one not agreeing, are enclosed in parentheses. Students need to identify the preferred verb. This done, the teacher "goes over" the exercise, and this experience is replicated under testing circumstances. Students get the grades they get, and the class moves on to pronoun-antecedent agreement matters.

What is accomplished? Not much. In the fluency of writing and speaking, students will not remember and apply the rule. There will be a maddening discrepancy between performance on the exercise or test and that which we see in the natural use of language.

And why do we use language in certain ways? We use language in the styles we do because our language use blends with others in our speech community. We trust our ears, and our ears are usually reliable. For those times when there is a discrepancy, we need intervention, not to "correct" us, but to bring into line what we will call the "standard" form and the "common" one.

The intervention (instruction, if you will) should be as matter-of-fact as possible, without condescension, exasperation, or insult. Remember that a student's manner of speaking the English language (or any native language, for that matter) arises from the student's home and community. Remember also that language is a changing, varying social agreement. And remember that you can learn about and from your students' language and culture as much as they can learn about and from yours. Build a swinging door, not a closed door, between your preferred and customary language style and that of your students.

That said, how best to intervene? I suggest posing a series of questions revolving around illustrative sentences:

1. Does this sound formal or informal?
2. If it sounds informal, who might say or write it this way?
3. What part of it sounds informal?
4. How would we code-switch this into formal English?
5. What is the rule?

The first four questions can be answered without any technical knowledge; the fifth requires understanding enough terminology to apply a grammatical rule.

Just as I had to learn the finer points of setting a formal table, our students need to learn the details of Standard Written English (SWE) (and Standard Spoken English [SSE] as well), inasmuch as those details vary from their vernacular. I couldn't have learned how to set a formal table without using the terminology (*wine glass, water tumbler, serving pieces*, etc.) and understanding the taxonomy (glasses, plates, silver-ware). My table-setting teacher would not have referred to a salad fork and a dinner fork as "this thing here" and "that thing there." She used the correct terminology in a natural context, and if I didn't understand, she explained without fanfare or much of a break in the task of setting the table. She apprenticed me to her, allowing me to do what she thought I was capable of, which was a little bit more than I thought I was ready to do. She explained the logic behind the rules, to the best of her knowledge. When she didn't know why something went here and not there, she simply said: "That's the tradition. That's what people expect when they come to dinner."

When we play a game, there are "official" rules and "house" rules. It's important to know the difference. A player who insists on playing as though every game is a tournament will be an unwelcome player anywhere but on the tournament circuit. A player who knows only informal, family-and-friends rules will be penalized (and embarrassed) at an official game.

In a 1981 article titled "Not All Errors Are Created Equal," Maxine Hairston discusses the degree of "bothersome-ness" that various "errors" have on readers who are professionals in fields other than education. Her work, known as "the Hairston study," establishes that some variations from SWE are highly disdained, while others, often scientifically very close to the highly disdained errors, are not considered bothersome. The most offensive variations/errors are those that characterize the writer as using a regional dialect. In other words, a high price is to be charged to those who don't observe code-switching expectations. Other high-price errors are the use of nonstandard verb forms in irregular verbs (*brung, brang*), double negatives, subject-verb mismatch (*he don't*) and, of course, the despised use of *ain't*.

Lists of detailed SWE rules are easy enough to find, and many curriculum guides have broken them down grade by grade in what they consider an effective scope and sequence. It is not our intention to turn this book into a handbook or to present such a scope and sequence for usage and mechanics. Instead, we offer the list below, as well as a breakdown of the grammatical rules that govern the items on high-stakes tests such as the SAT. The scope and sequence we offer in Chapter 8 is more conceptually based than error based, we're pleased to say.

Error-based grammar instruction tends to fall from its own weight. Despite earnest efforts to build a grammar curriculum that will zap errors from the face of a school district once and for all, most English teachers despair at finding the same old mistakes again and again.

We propose a different paradigm, one that is strength based rather than error based: Use exemplary writing—student writing and professional writing—to build skills. Teach students to notice what strong writers do well rather than what weak writers do badly. Here is a list of rules and guidelines for clear and accurate writing. We've developed these rules and guidelines from the writing of our students, using positive, encouraging statements.

Rules and Guidelines for Clear and Accurate Writing

1. **The Rule of Diction:** Choose words that are suited to the context and audience. This will allow your reader to take you seriously.

2. **The Rule of Joining Independent Clauses:** We need more than just a comma to join two independent clauses. To join independent clauses to each other, we need either a semicolon or a comma along with a coordinating conjunction. Observing this rule will allow your reader to understand where your ideas begin and end and will eliminate confusion.

3. **The Rule of Proximity:** Place all grammatical structures next to what they modify. This will allow your readers to see how your words relate to one another and will eliminate confusion.

4. **The Rule of Complete Sentences:** To test whether a group of words constitutes a complete sentence, try tacking a tag question to it. Then try transforming the group of words into a question that is answerable by *yes* or *no*. Complete sentences can pass both of these tests.

5. **The Rule of Apostrophes:** Use apostrophes to signify possessives and contractions. There is no apostrophe in the word *its* when used as a possessive pronoun.

6. **The Rule of Hyphenation:** Hyphenate compound adjectives. That is, hyphenate adjectives that are formed out of a noun and a participle, such as *fish-eating bird* or *moth-eaten sweater*. Observing this rule will eliminate confusion.

7. **The Rules of Agreement:**

    a. Subject-verb: The subject and the verb must agree. Both must be singular or both must be plural. Most of the time, if a prepositional phrase intervenes between the subject and the verb (*A box of matches is on the table*), we disregard the prepositional phrase in matching the subject to the verb. Sometimes, however, such as when the subject is *some*, as in *Some of the pie was eaten; Some of the cookies were left over*, it is the noun after the preposition that is matched to the verb.

    b. Pronoun-antecedent: All pronouns refer to something that comes before them somewhere in the text. The thing or concept that the pronoun refers to is called the *antecedent*. The pronoun must agree with its antecedent. Because English has no generic singular pronoun, we run into a problem in sentences such as *Everybody is to bring ___own lunch*. What you can do is what some editors call *RTA* ("revise to avoid" this dilemma). Thus, *All campers are to bring their own lunches*. The traditional, now outdated, style that I learned in school back in the fifties and sixties was to use "he/his/him" as the default singular pronoun. Now most publishers (including NCTE) require nonsexist, or bias-free, language: the writer is advised to recast the sentence using a plural antecedent so that the singular *they* dilemma is avoided. In *Revising the Rules*, Brock Haussamen explains that it wasn't until the mid-eighteenth century that the preferred use of the singular masculine pronoun as the generic form was codified. Says Haussamen, "The first explicit definition of the sex indefinite *he* appeared in 1746 in the grammar of J. Kirby: 'Rule 21: The masculine Person answers to the general Name, which comprehends both Male and Female'" (100). Thus began this particular example of male bias on the part of traditional grammarians. The use of *he or she* generally calls unnecessary attention to itself, and that is why we arrive at the solution of simply recasting the sentence (or RTA) to smooth out the sentence and not offend either the strict traditionalists or those who bristle at sexist language.

8. **The Rule of Pronoun Case:** Use the correct case (subjective or objective) of pronouns. We don't usually have a problem when there's only one pronoun in a structure: *I saw a great movie. Ask me about it*. But we sometimes run into a problem when we add another person: *Judi and I saw a great movie. If you have any questions, ask her or me*. This, as opposed to **Judi and me saw a great movie. If you have any questions about it, ask her or I*. Remember: The object should be in the objective case. Your reader will appreciate your attention to detail.

9. **The Guidelines of Commas:** Remember LIES:

   L: Lists. The comma before the final item in a series is optional.

   I: Introductions. Place a comma before elements that precede the subject. If the element is shorter than five words, and if the element would not cause confusion, then the comma is optional. If the introductory element includes a verb, then the comma is required.

   E: Extra Information. Divide extra (nonessential) information of all kinds with a comma on each side.

> **S: Side-by-Side Sentences.** Separate independent clauses (sentences) with a comma and a conjunction. (Note: Also, observe the comma rules that apply to quotations.)

Your reader will appreciate observance of comma rules because commas prevent word collisions that result in confusion. Unnecessary commas impede comprehension.

TEACHER'S JOURNAL

Today's lesson is about code-switching, a grammatical concept my students encounter and employ every day. I feel confident about the concept but uneasy about the myriad directions the topic may take us. To control the uncertainty, I leave the initial discussion open and structure the activity around our current text, *The Scarlet Letter*. As the students enter, I'm playing a track off the latest Beck CD, *Guero*, hoping that later, students will connect his witty, flexible use of Spanglish, Ebonics, and other urban dialects to our discussion.

I open the lesson with some questions about language. I find the students eager to discuss how they speak and write in different situations depending on audience.

"Let's say you are in the cafeteria. You are talking with your friends about a trip to the mall. Maybe you bought some new clothes; maybe you saw some cute boys, or girls; maybe you picked up some new tunes. . . . How does the language you use to speak with them differ from the way you speak to your teachers, parents, or grandparents? Do you have a different vocabulary? Do you phrase your statements differently? And where do such phrases come from?"

A few comments are negative but nonetheless productive.

"I don't know how I talk; I never analyze it."

"Fair enough," I reply, "but we're analyzing it now, and you might be surprised what you discover."

John offers, "We shorten everything—language is getting stupider."

"Do you have any idea why that is happening, John?"

"I guess time is more valuable. Things happen so quickly now."

Ryan is excited to respond. "We just say what comes naturally. We use a lot of slang and we all talk at the same time, but we understand each other."

"Interesting. So you don't talk to me the same way?" I ask, hoping to expand on his comments.

"Well, no. We use more slang; it's more informal."

"So you adapt your language to your audience?"

"Yeah, we don't want to sound rude when we're speaking to you. And we don't want to use words that you don't understand."

"Well, that's very respectful of you, Ryan. But would you be surprised to learn that I do the same thing? When I'm hanging out with my friends, I switch codes to communicate more effectively, just like you. Sometimes I incorporate words and phrases from my cultural experiences with music and movies and travel."

We're on our way. I can sense the energy in the room building. The students are curious about codes because language patterns give them a sense of identity. I continue the discussion by writing some instant messaging (IM) acronyms on the board:

LOL   BRB   JK   ROTFL   PLZ

I keep it simple, knowing they can blow me away with their expertise on the subject. I ask the students to interpret each abbreviation, and before I know it we're laughing and talking openly about the variety of Internet language at their disposal. Not wanting the concept to be lost, I write a definition of code-switching on the board: *Code-switching* is a term in linguistics referring to alternation between two or more languages, dialects, or language registers in the course of discourse between people who have more than one language in common. Sometimes the switch lasts only for a few sentences, or even for a single phrase. This definition is just one I pulled off the Wikipedia website, but it serves our discussion well. I ask the students to copy it into the grammar section of their notebooks. Melanie, bright-eyed and curious, raises her hand.

"I didn't think about it that way, but it makes sense. You must have a common language, but then you adapt it, depending on who you're talking to."

Lisa chimes in, "Like when we're online, Mel."

Jordan's in on it too: "Like when we talk like gangsta rappers because of the music we listen to."

I can't resist getting involved, showing off my code knowledge.

"That's what I'm talking about, yo. But you gotta be cool, hombre; you can't rap wit Grams dat way. You gotta be chill wit da choices, dig? Y' knows what I'm sayin."

They're all laughing now, but we're driving the concept home. I let Emilio add a final comment.

"When I visit my cousins in the Bronx, I change the way I speak. Sometimes it's hard to switch back when I come home."

I know that we could talk about this for days. It doesn't feel like learning. This is what good lessons look like: real, relevant, relaxed, and alive!

With the introduction solidified and the enthusiasm peaked, I move on. I ask the students to break out their *Scarlet Letter* novels and find a partner. I've made a handout with the definition of code-switching at the top and two columns underneath. I ask the students to write three to five lines of dialogue from the novel on one side and on the other side a modern interpretation using IM language. Some students are eager to try other dialects, and I allow them without hesitation, gently warning them to avoid derogatory or inappropriate language.

They have many questions as they begin. And I realize that the activity will require some clarification and assistance.

"Can we use misspellings?"

"Yes, but be conscious of why you're making them."

"Do we have to use a conversation, or can we pull lines from various places?"

"You can use any dialogue you wish, but it might be easier to focus on a specific conversation for context."

Before long the class is immersed in language analysis and interpretation. I know they're getting into it when I hear, "Oh, we're gonna make screen names for Hester and Dimmesdale!" I wander the room listening in, keeping the groups on task. As the groups finish their work, I ask them to write a short paragraph explaining what they learned about the differences in language. Here are some of their responses.

"Even though I'm IMing, I still use a lot of commas. They help to show pauses when someone isn't right in front of you."

"We had to switch word order around a lot. Phrases are backwards and we use more double negatives."

"Thanks to computers, we can use smiley faces to show emotion, without using words. Technology affects language; it makes communication easy."

"The message stays the same, but it's much more informal."

"We have new words, and many of the words have disappeared."

"It seems like we don't express our thoughts as clearly, and there are less allusions to religion."

"The rules aren't as strict."

"Back then, language was a way to express intelligence—a status symbol. That's not the case now."

We use the final minutes of the period to discuss their conclusions. It's a smart conversation, and I'm relieved that they grasp the intricacies of code-switching so well. We don't get a chance to get back to Beck, but I know future grammar discourse will benefit from our work today. Following is one of their interpretations.

Original

"Trust me, good jailor, you shall briefly have peace in your house; and, I promise you Mistress Prynne shall hereafter be more amenable to just authority than you have found her heretofore."

IM Interpretation

"Trust me man. It's gonna be peaceful in your crib + I'm tellin' ya—ur motha Prynne be's good now + follows her peeps laws."

NCTE's Resolution: Students' Right to Their Own Language

We conclude this chapter on usage and mechanics issues with some reflections on NCTE's landmark document "Students' Right to Their Own Language." In 1974, NCTE issued a resolution known as "On the Students' Right to Their Own Language." The long document on which this resolution is based was reaffirmed in 2003 and updated in 2006.

Resolution

Resolved, that the National Council of Teachers of English affirm the students' right to their own language—to the dialect that expresses their family and community identity, the idiolect that expresses their unique personal identity;

that NCTE affirm the responsibility of all teachers of English to assist all students in the development of their ability to speak and write better whatever their dialects;

that NCTE affirm the responsibility of all teachers to provide opportunities for clear and cogent expression of ideas in writing, and to provide the opportunity for students to learn the conventions of what has been called written edited American English; and

that NCTE affirm strongly that teachers must have the experiences and training that will enable them to understand and respect diversity of dialects.

Be it further Resolved, that, to this end,

that NCTE make available to other professional organizations this resolution as well as suggestions for ways of dealing with linguistic variety, as expressed in the CCCC background statement on students' right to their own language; and

that NCTE promote classroom practices to expose students to the variety of dialects that comprise our multiregional, multiethnic, and multicultural society, so that they too will understand the nature of American English and come to respect all its dialects.

The kind of grammar instruction this book promotes is not antithetical to the resolution. Every time we open our mouths to speak, we are speaking a dialect. The prestige dialect, the dialect of privilege, is Standard English. Standard Spoken English is less formal than Standard Written English. English is not the only language to have a prestige dialect: French has its Parisian dialect; Spanish, its Castilian.

If we teach students whose home dialect is markedly different from the prestige dialect, then the job is to teach these students two things. The first is to code-switch into the prestige dialect. The second, on which the first depends, is to teach them the systematic nature of their home dialect. Students who speak a rural dialect, or black vernacular English, or a working-class urban dialect are likely to hold the same negative attitudes that those in more prestigious precincts of society believe about such dialects: that they are unsystematic, "broken" English, inferior in expressiveness to the prestige dialects. When students have such negative ideas about their own voices and those of their families, neighbors, and friends, we should not be surprised to find them embarrassed to participate in any language activities in school, especially those that involve writing, a permanent visible sign of one's language use.

John Rickford of Stanford University has championed pedagogy that builds on the students' vernacular to teach code-switching into the prestige dialect. Rickford defended the Oakland (California) School Board's decision to train teachers in the systems of African American Vernacular English (AAVE) (also called Ebonics) so they could teach students to code-switch. Says Rickford in *The San Jose Mercury News*:

> Over three decades, both in this country and abroad (e.g., Sweden), show that teaching methods which DO take vernacular dialects into account in teaching the standard work better than those which DO NOT. For instance, Hanni Taylor, in a 1989 book entitled *Standard English, Black English, and Bidialectalism*, reported that he tried to improve the Standard English writing of inner city university students from Chicago using two methods. With the experimental group, he raised students' metalinguistic awareness of the differences between Ebonics and Standard English through contrastive analysis, and tailored pattern practice drills. With the control group, he did not do this, but simply followed "traditional English department techniques." After nearly three months of instruction, the experimental group showed a 59% reduction in the use of Ebonics features in their SE writing, while the control group, using traditional methods, showed a slight INCREASE (8.5%) in the use of AAVE features.

Similar studies with supporting results have been conducted in New-port News, Virginia, by Rebecca Wheeler and Rachel Swords, and out of Stanford University by Julie Sweetland.

Studying the differences between dialects, feature by feature, is an effective and exciting way to teach grammar. This method is called contrastive analysis. In contrastive analysis, students simply place sentences from two dialects (one being Standard English) side by side. They draw conclusions about the rules demonstrated by each of the dialects, just as a scientific observer would do when analyzing data.

In my Semantics and Rhetoric class, most of the students speak a dialect that is fairly close to Standard English. This doesn't mean they don't need to learn about other dialects. For them to learn true respect for and understanding of other cultures, they need to be educated out of their language prejudices, prejudices that are deeply embedded in our society and that are assumed to be not prejudices, but justifiable preferences for the "better" dialect.

Recently, I was teaching a series of lessons about the sentence patterns. We came to the pattern in which verbs take indirect objects. In the standard dialect, the verbs that do this are verbs of giving and showing:

> I gave my brother a ticket to the Jets game.
>
> I showed Alex my new car.

This is Standard English usage, but various regional American dialects use indirect objects for other verbs:

> He married him a girl from Oklahoma City.
>
> I'm going to climb me a tree.
>
> I'm going to have me a doughnut.

Through literature and by listening to real language, students can learn to describe dialect features in grammatical terms.

6 Grammar and Standardized Tests

The purpose of this chapter is to explore ways in which our grammar instruction can elevate student performance on standardized tests, including gatekeeping exams such as the SAT and ACT. But "teaching to the test" is not our goal. The demands of an institutionalized, high-stakes test should not dictate our decisions as educators. Rather, we need to understand the nature of the tests that our students face and fret about. Once we understand what the tests are asking for in terms of grammar, we need to find ways to improve the requisite skills gracefully, and without compromising what we know to be meaningful classroom experiences. I believe it is possible to do this.

The on-demand essay is addressed fully in other books such as *Writing Put to the Test: Teaching for the High Stakes Essay* (Benjamin) and *Writing on Demand: Best Practices and Strategies for Success* (Gere, Christenbury, and Sassi). In this book, I limit the discussion to the knowledge about grammar that is needed for short-answer questions. Beginning in 2005, the SAT included what is called a "writing skills segment" as well as an on-demand essay. The writing skills segment would more accurately be called "editing" because the test-taker needs to respond to text as an editor would, discerning effective and felicitous sentences from those that may be nonstandard, unclear, wordy, or unnecessarily taxing on the reader. Both of these tasks have appeared before on the SAT II, ACT, and PSAT.

Where does grammar fit in? To write a coherent and cogent essay, obviously, the student must be fluent in Standard Written English. As I've stated throughout this book, achieving that fluency comes as a result of consistent, developmentally appropriate instruction in all of the traits of writing: focus, development, organization, language (diction and syntax), and the surface features of writing such as spelling, punctuation, capitalization, agreement, parallelism, verb formation, and other manifestations of standard usage.

As for the short-answer segment, much of the skill required to do the editing will be developed in the course of becoming an effective writer through the writing process. Through process, students learn to test out their sentences on readers, finding out if their syntax is clear and kind to the reader. The writer may discover that the reader is confused in places where pronoun-antecedent connections need to be clarified. Or the writer may find that a sentence rambles or gets tangled up in verbiage. Through process, writers compose trial sentences that they may read aloud or hear others read aloud to them. We often find that a sentence that isn't "kind to the mouth" (doesn't "read aloud" well) can be streamlined. And through process, writers trim and groom their words, training the sentences within a paragraph to fall into line. Parallel structure creates order and facilitates comprehension, and parallel structure is coaxed out of unruly sentences as the writer rewrites. Although writing process instruction takes a primary place in effective writing programs, we need to supplement it with explicit instruction in sentence crafting.

The debate over the extent to which instruction is enhanced or diminished by the demands of high-stakes tests is not the focus of this book. That is a matter that will continue to be debated while the Age of Testing runs its course. Meanwhile, we have students who desire entrance into the colleges of their choice. Many of these students can afford test-prep classes and even private tutors to maximize their chances. Indeed, in many circles, such training is de rigueur, every bit as expected as the ritualistic family outings to visit colleges during the months preceding the student's senior year of high school. But not every student has a family in a position to provide such things. Should those students not receive an equal chance in the SAT game?

Once we acknowledge that our misgivings about the justice and educational value of the SAT and its ilk should not keep our less well-heeled students out of the colleges of their choice, we need to settle in to helping students succeed on such tests. So first, let's have a look at the kinds of questions the writing skills segment of the SAT serves up. Then we will analyze the skills that test-takers need in order to answer these questions. After that, we will propose some ways these skills can be taught in keeping with the pedagogically sound learning experiences we've promoted in this book.

The short-answer grammar segment has three kinds of questions: (1) identification of errors, (2) sentence correction, and (3) editing in context.

The first kind of question, identification of error, presents a sentence that has certain words and phrases underlined. The test-taker must identify which part of the sentence has an error. The test-taker is *not* required to name the error, nor to correct it. The test items look like this:

Jenna <u>missed</u> the train this <u>morning because</u> her <u>husband who</u>
      a.   b.   c.

always drops her off at the <u>Huntington Station,</u> never came
home last night due to the massive blackout, <u>which</u> we've all
                                                  d.

heard about. <u>No error.</u>
              e.

 The test-taker would be expected to identify C as the answer here because of the missing comma. But the test-taker would not be expected
to name the error as "lack of comma to set off a nonrestrictive element."
A fastidious reader might not like the use of "due to" or that the sentence ends in a preposition. But those parts of the sentence are not up
for grabs.

The second question type, sentence correction, presents a sentence
in which a part (or all) is underlined. The test-taker must discern if the
underlined part is the best possible way to express the intended idea.
The choices given are alternate ways of expressing that idea. Such test
items look like this:

<u>Tim Becker amazes us with his mathematical ability, I think</u> it's
true to say that he's never miscalculated a single problem.

    (a) Tim Becker amazes us with his mathematical ability, I
          think

    (b) Tim Becker amazes us with his mathematical ability and
          I think

    (c) Tim Becker who amazes us with mathematical ability, I
          think

    (d) Tim Becker amazes us with his mathematical ability. I
          think

The best answer is D because the two independent clauses demand to
be properly separated. Choice A is a comma splice; B is a run-on because
there is no comma before the coordinating conjunction *and* in this compound sentence; and C is the same as A (still a comma splice, and the
omission of *his* doesn't help the situation). Note that choice A is always
the "as is" choice. It is possible that the presenting sentence is correct
as is. Note also that the test-taker is *not* required to name the error, but
only to sense the syntax that adheres most closely to formal Standard
Written English.

The third question type, editing in context, presents a draft of an
essay. The component sentences are numbered. This is the most com-

prehensive of the three question types. The test-taker may be asked to identify a weakness in the style, to judge whether the sentences follow in the most coherent order, or to determine whether any words should be changed to achieve agreement (although the word *agreement* is not used in either the question or the answer). This question type may look like this:

> (1) The natural world depends upon biodiversity for stability. (2) Ecologists know the importance of biodiversity, and that is why they urge scientific interventions in agricultural practices to control population growth in certain species that tend to destabilize the ecosystem. (3) Just as diversity ensures stability in the natural world, diversity ensures stability in the human world. (4) Therefore, as we move closer and closer to being a "global village," maybe we should think about whether we are losing our diversity. (5) If everyone speaks the same language, eats the same food, wears the same clothes, what diversity will we have? (6) Will the fact that everyone is the same promote peace or will it accomplish the opposite? (7) If the ecologists are right, then the answer is the latter. (8) Sure, it sounds good to have a world where everyone can communicate with each other via one language. (9) But wouldn't "one world" be uninteresting to travel in? (10) Part of the fascination of this great big beautiful world of ours is that we are different cultures.

The questions might require the test-taker to discern that:

> 1. The language tone is a bit informal, and phrasing such as "Sure, it sounds good . . . ," as well as the informality of sentences 8–10, might be too casual if the intended audience is a teacher expecting an academic tone.
>
> 2. Rhetorical questions are used to make key points, expressing the opinion of the writer.
>
> 3. The writer uses a sentence-to-sentence transition in sentence 4 (i.e., *Therefore*). (Note: Items 2 and 3 are positive features of the paragraph.)
>
> 4. The writer does not provide specific examples.
>
> 5. The writer may want to consider dividing this discourse into at least two paragraphs.

The "editing in context" questions are clearly the ones that simulate the writing process most authentically. This is because the sentences are presented in the context of paragraphs rather than as isolated sentences. Therefore, these would be the easiest questions to embed in the natural course of process instruction. Even so, the teacher with an eye toward student success on the SAT would do well to know the kinds of questions and the language that the SAT test-makers use. Such language includes the following terms:

Writer's style

Writer's tone

Parallel structure

Reliance on general statements

Analogy

Choice of verb tense

Inconsistent verb tense

Lack of agreement

Rhetorical

Narrative; personal narrative

General to specific

Specific to general

Pronoun usage

Diction

Transition

Contradiction

To help you orient your instruction around the kinds of grammar skills that students need for the SAT, here are categorized examples of the kinds of sentences that appear on the grammar segment of the SAT:

- Comma use or misuse
- Idiom and diction
- Semicolon use and misuse
- Verb forms
- Pronoun case and number
- Verb tense or subject-verb agreement
- Parallel structure
- Placement of elements within the sentence
- Comparison

Comma Use or Misuse

Expect to see comma splices, commas omitted from nonrestrictive elements, and commas omitted where they should be separating an introductory element from the subject of the sentence. Expect to see commas inserted where there should be no comma, particularly between the required slots of a sentence: subject and verb, verb and direct object.

Students are often taught to rely on their intuition when it comes to comma placement, but it is exactly where their intuition is likely to be *wrong* that they will see comma errors, such as in a comma splice. Better advice is to teach the basic set of comma rules. Train students to have a *known reason* for inserting a comma:

> **L:** Commas to separate items in a list (the series comma)
>
> **I:** Commas to set off introductions (the introductory element comma before the subject, the direct address comma)
>
> **E:** Commas to set off extra information (the nonrestrictive element comma pair, the appositive comma pair)
>
> **S:** Commas to set off side-by-side sentences when a coordinating conjunction is also used (the compound sentence comma)

(You may want to refer to Chapter 5 if you need a more comprehensive explanation of the LIES comma rules.)

In addition to the LIES commas, you can add the comma rules that apply to quotations and those that apply to conventional situations such as city and state, day of month and year, after salutations and closings in letters, between a person's name and a suffix such as Jr. (the comma is optional, according to *The Chicago Manual of Style*, 15th Edition; the writer is advised to be consistent) or PhD.

Chief pitfalls in comma use are in reversals and compound verbs.

Reversals

Commas can signify that something is out of order. For example, the usual order of clauses in a complex sentence would have the main clause preceding the subordinate clause. When we choose to lead with the subordinate clause, we treat it as an introductory element, thus separating it from the main clause with a comma:

1. Ron Howard was once a child star but is now a highly reputed film director. (normal order)
2. A former child star, Ron Howard is now a highly reputed film director. (reversal)

Compound Verbs

It's an easy mistake to insert a comma in sentences in which one subject governs two verbs, because such a sentence resembles a compound sentence. Thus:

*Humpty Dumpty sat on a wall, and had a great fall.
Humpty Dumpty sat on a wall and had a great fall.

To teach comma use, replicate some authentic text you find in literature or the newspaper. *Remove all commas*, but tell the students how many commas should be used in the excerpt. This is their comma allowance. Then have students spend their comma allowance, giving the reason for the expenditure of each comma. This learning experience differs from the traditional comma-placement exercise in which students read a rule and then apply that rule to a list of artificial sentences presented to illustrate that rule.

Because of the nature of syntax, it's important to distinguish between comma pairs and single commas. This distinction will help students understand that comma pairs set off subordinating elements or modifiying structures from the foregrounded parts of the sentence. When we think of parts of the sentence as being in the background or in the foreground, we create a mental three-dimensional picture of the sentence that will improve reading comprehension as we understand what is important and what is secondary.

A way to blend comma teaching with literary interpretation is to remove the commas from a Shakespearean monologue and have students insert the commas, giving a reason for each. To do this, the students really have to think about meaning in text. Here is what it might look like if students have a comma allowance of five (two pairs; one single):

Commas omitted:

> *Viola:* There is a fair behavior in thee captain
> And though that nature with a beauteous wall
> Doth oft close in pollution yet of thee
> I will believe thou hast a mind that suits
> With this thy fair and outward character.
> I prithee and I'll pay thee bounteously
> Conceal me what I am and be my aid
> For such disguise as haply shall become
> The form of my intent. I'll serve this duke.

Commas restored and explained:

> *Viola:* There is a fair behavior in thee, captain,
> And though that nature with a beauteous wall
> Doth oft close in pollution, yet of thee
> I will believe thou hast a mind that suits
> With this thy fair and outward character.

I prithee, and I'll pay thee bounteously,
Conceal me what I am, and be my aid
For such disguise as haply shall become
The form of my intent. I'll serve this duke.

When the commas are inserted, the reader receives direction in how to read the passage with the right pacing and emphasis. The comma pairs establish dimension, directing the reader/actor to adjust pitch and volume to clarify meaning and simulate the cadences of speech.

Idiom and Diction

On the SAT grammar section, we find items that are not really about grammar but about idiom and diction. This can come under the general heading of "usage." Items of this type may look like this:

1. *The reason I never responded to your wedding invitation is because I never received it, probably due to a change in address which had been inaccurately reported.

Here, the student is expected to know that the test-makers do not like the diction in "the reason is because," although this is very commonly heard diction. The test-makers want to hear "the reason is *that*." They may not want to hear "due to" either. There are still some Strunk and White purists who would insist on "owing to"!

2. *There cannot be less than thirty students in a class; more than thirty students wouldn't fit comfortably in the classroom.

Here, the student is expected to know that the word *fewer* and not the word *less* is the preferred standard use when matched with countable nouns.

3. *The psychological affects of addiction can be just as compelling as the physical ones.

And here is the dreaded *affect/effect* distinction. Almost always, *affect* will be the verb and *effect* the noun. Confusion arises because there are times when *effect* can be used as a verb to mean "to bring about," as in *Increased industrialization effected a change in the air quality*. *Affect*, as a verb, means "influence," which is extremely close in meaning to what *effect* means as a verb, and therein lies the confusion when we teach both uses of *effect* at the same time. I recommend the shortcut of teaching *affect* as the verb and *effect* as the noun, saving *effect* as verb for those who have some chance of understanding it. If your students learned to use *affect* as the verb and *effect* as the noun, they have about a 98 percent chance of being correct. If you confuse them, you're back to a 50 percent chance, or worse.

The preceding three pitfalls are very likely to appear on the SAT, because they are transitional in the language and thus used in nonstandard ways often enough to indicate the extent to which students hit the mark of the register of English that is expected in academic discourse. I suggest teaching these idiom-diction items in a straightforward manner that includes a discussion of language use as a status marker.

Semicolon Use and Misuse

When the semicolon is used incorrectly (which it so often is, even by educated people), the mistake is usually the presentation of a dependent clause, rather than an independent clause, following the semicolon. For some reason, this is an elusive concept to many writers. I think it is an unlearned concept because it is an *untaught* one. For example:

> *No one can doubt the depth of her commitment to our organization; generous contributions, tireless service, meticulous attention to detail, and limitless patience.

Typically, the writer here has used a semicolon where a colon is called for to introduce a list that supplies examples to justify an assertion.

You can teach the semicolon the same way that I suggested you teach commas. Editorials, particularly, use a lot of semicolons (which tells you something about their usefulness and their air of formality). Give students text in which semicolons have been removed. Give them a semicolon allowance and have them supply the missing semicolons. To do this, they will need to be able to identify closely related independent clauses.

In addition to joining closely related independent clauses, semicolons have another job: they separate items in a series when the items themselves contain commas. However, this use of the semicolon is not usually an item in the SAT grammar section.

Verb Forms

Most of the transgressions in verb form use that you'll see on the SAT are those involving the past perfect tense. (Many experts refer to only two tenses in English: past and present. These experts would refer to what I am calling the past perfect *tense* as the past perfect *aspect*. I am here using the term *tense* because I assume that *tense* will be more familiar to you than *aspect*.)

> *If the snow had began earlier, there would have been no school today.

To teach how the simple past, present perfect, and past perfect tenses are used, show examples from narratives that are meant to be read by fourth- and fifth-grade students, such as *Charlotte's Web* or the other E. B. White novels. In them, you'll find lots of easily explainable examples of multiple, complex tenses, such as this:

> Darkness settled over everything. Soon there were only shadows and the noises of the sheep chewing their cuds, and occasionally the rattle of a cow-chain up overhead. You can imagine Wilbur's surprise when, out of the darkness, came a small voice he had never heard before. (31)

You can also try Harry Potter literature:

> Snow was swirling against the icy windows once more; Christmas was approaching fast. Hagrid had already single-handedly delivered the usual twelve Christmas trees for the Great Hall; garlands of holly and tinsel had been twisted around the banisters of the stairs; everlasting candles glowed from inside the helmets of suits of armor and great bunches of mistletoe had been hung at intervals along the corridors. (Rowling 303)

To teach these concepts using authentic literature, simply write the sentences on the board, indicate the verbs, and engage students in a discussion of the meanings and implications of tenses: What is the order in which things happened? What things were happening simultaneously? How do we know?

Pronoun Case and Number

English has three pronoun cases—subjective, objective, and possessive—and the chief interest among them, according to test-makers, is the use of the objective case (*me, us; him, her, them*) in the subject slot and in the predicate nominative slot. For some odd reason, test-makers generally show little if any concern for the reverse. That is, when people say "between you and I," using the subjective case as the object of a preposition, the error often goes unnoticed even by educated people. The use of a subjective case pronoun instead of an objective case pronoun is not a status-marking error; the use of the objective case pronoun instead of a subjective case pronoun *is* a status-marking error, and you can count on it being a test item. Expect to see items like these:

> *While us sopranos were singing the second refrain, no one noticed that our director had just given the signal to skip to the final section.

The test-taker is expected to recognize that the called-for pronoun would be *we*, as this pronoun functions as the subject.

> *No one knew that Johnson and me were the low bidders.

Here, we can use the "take the other one out" trick: no native speaker would use the objective case if Johnson weren't in the picture, as in:

> *No one knew that me was the low bidder.

> There's a chance, of course, that the test-makers will pull the reverse, seeing if the test-taker really does know their pronouns. I did this on purpose. You recognized, of course, the mismatch that results from using the plural *their* with the singular *test-taker*. Time was, the generic singular pronoun was supposed to be in the masculine gender, hence:

> *There's a chance, of course, that the test-maker will pull the reverse, seeing if the test-taker really does know his pronouns.

But today, most publishers have style guides disallowing sexist language. So what's a poor girl to do? The easiest way out of this thicket is simply to pluralize the referent:

> There's a chance, of course, that the test maker will pull the reverse, seeing if the test-takers really do know their pronouns.

Problem solved. As mentioned in Chapter 5, many editors suggest using RTA, which stands for "revise to avoid." Fortunately, the English language offers multiple ways to say something, so it's not that difficult to crawl out of a grammatical hole.

> Anyway, you might see something like this on the SAT:

> *Between you and I, I can't understand why Sylvia got the promotion, rather than Miriam.

Relatedly, you might find the subjective case pronoun used where the objective case is called for, as in:

> *If you have any questions, see Joe or I.

> Now, *who* versus *whom*. Although *whom* is phasing out of the language, it is alive and well in standardized tests of English usage. You'll find:

> *We finally discovered whom had committed the murder in the ballroom with the lead pipe.

Who, as the subjective case pronoun, goes wherever *I, we, he, she,* and *they* can go. *Whom*, as the objective case pronoun, goes wherever *me, us, him, her,* and *them* can go. Try this: A *who/whom* sentence often implies a question. That question can be answered with either *he* or *him* (*she* or *her*, if you prefer. See above.) Here's how it works. In the preceding example, the implied question would be answered like this: *He (she) had committed the murder in the ballroom with the lead pipe.* Therefore, since a subjective case pronoun would be used to answer the implied question, we need *who*:

> We finally discovered who had committed the murder in the ballroom with the lead pipe.

Consider this sentence: *Because of who we are and whom we serve, we are mindful of our duties.* We use *who* in *who we are* because the linking verb (*are*) requires the subjective case (*we*); we use *whom* in *whom we serve* because the action verb (*serve*) requires the objective case (*whom*). Because the difference might not be easy to understand, let me explain it further: When you have a linking verb, that which follows the linking verb refers to the same referent as the subject of the sentence and therefore is in the subjective case. When we say *who we are*, there is but one referent (*we*). The *who* refers to *we*, and therefore both are in the same case (subjective). When we have an action verb, however, that which follows the action verb, its direct object, is a different referent: When we say *whom we serve*, the *whom* refers to *them*. *We* are different from *them*.

The temptation may be to teach the concept and then get busy with some exercises in the grammar book. That will result, counterintuitively enough, in perfection on the exercises with no transfer to authentic situations. Instead, I'm recommending what I always recommend: Use authentic text to illustrate this concept as you run into it naturally, in the course of reading and speech.

Verb Tense or Subject-Verb Agreement:

Expect to see problems with the use of the subjunctive mood, as in:

> *If I <u>was</u> in your shoes, I'd be able to leap tall buildings in a single bound.

The "if" clause should set off an alarm. Many English speakers rarely hear the subjunctive (the form of the verb that is used to indicate conditions that are contrary to fact, as in *If I were you*) used in this manner, so this is one usage that should be explicitly taught in anticipation of this kind of test item.

In matters of subject-verb agreement, we have to take out the intervening prepositional phrase(s) to discern how the subject sounds with the verb. A typical test item will look like this:

> *One <u>of the candles</u> were left lit.

When we disregard the intervening prepositional phrase, we easily see that we need the singular form of the verb: *One . . . candle <u>was</u> left lit.*
Similarly, but seemingly harder to see, is this one:

> *Not one of the committee members were able to run for president of the organization, so we made the decision to divide up the tasks among the seven members and divided up the stipend as well.

Again, removing the intervening prepositional phrase highlights the disconnect between subject and verb: *Not one . . . <u>was</u> able to run for president of the organization, . . .*

Parallel Structure

Parallel structure, an important and ubiquitous feature of coherent syntax and style, is worth teaching for reasons even beyond the test.

1. *Madison's college essay is about what she expects to learn from playing intramural volleyball, studying child psychology, and to join an academically oriented sorority.

This sentence is not written with proper parallel structure, because the writer has two gerunds (*playing, studying*) mismatched with an infinitive (*to join*). Change *to join* to *joining* and the sentence works.

2. *I consider <u>Othello</u> and <u>Hamlet</u>, both of which have been made into film versions, to be not only enjoyable to theatergoers but also to history buffs.

Here, the sentence lacks proper parallelism because of the misplacement of the *not only/but also* correlatives. The sentence should read:

> I consider <u>Othello</u> and <u>Hamlet</u>, both of which have been made into film versions, to be enjoyable not only to theatergoers, but also to history buffs.

3. *To be an expert dancer, you have to possess a good sense of rhythm, an ability to improvise, and to anticipate the moves and direction of your partner.

Here there are three objects of the verb *possess*: two are noun phrases and the third is a verb phrase. All three should be noun phrases: *. . . and an anticipatory sense of the moves and direction of your partner.*

Teaching parallel structure as part of your writing instruction will make students better writers. A meaningful way to do this is through models. If you examine well-written text, you will find that more and more parallel structure emerges the closer you look at the piece. You'll find it from one paragraph to the next, among sentences, among clauses within sentences, and among phrases within clauses.

Placement

The dangling modifier has long been a staple in tests of this kind. The idea is that when a modifier strays from that which it modifies, confusion results. In actual fact, confusion does *not* always result, because the reader can usually sense the intended meaning and does not assume that an absurdity is true. Nevertheless, such modifiers are distracting to readers—and they detract from the writer's authority. You can expect to see this kind of test item:

> *With his nose pressed against the living room window, and with his little tail waggling, Timmy waved good-bye to his little pet dachshund, and off he went on his first day of kindergarten.

Obviously, Timmy is not pressing his nose to the window nor waggling his tail—his pet dachshund is.

You won't see dangling modifiers in authentic text for obvious reasons. The best way to teach students to spot them—and avoid them in their own writing—is by creating humorous sentences that derive their amusement value from the misplaced modifier.

Comparison

Here is another error that may, in fact, bother very few people in real life but that test-makers throw into the mix.

> *Some people believe that Chaucer's storytelling ability is superior to Shakespeare.

The test-maker is expecting the test-taker to recognize that Chaucer's storytelling ability cannot be compared to Shakespeare himself, but only to Shakespeare's storytelling ability. The sentence should be structured thus:

> Some people believe that Chaucer's storytelling ability is superior to that of Shakespeare.

Here's another, more subtle, example:

> *Atlanta's Hartfield Airport, judging by surface area only, is larger
> than any airport in the United States.

Because Hartfield Airport cannot be bigger than itself, the test-taker is
expected to want this:

> Atlanta's Hartfield Airport, judging by surface area only, is larger
> than any other airport in the United States.

And, finally, we have the difference between how we express comparison between two of something and comparison when there is more than
two:

> *Although I am the older of my three sisters, people tell me that I
> look like the youngest.

This item slyly tests whether the test-taker knows to use -*est* and not -*er*
for comparisons of more than two.

Students need time and practice to absorb this information, so a
brief cramming session before the test would be ineffective. Students
need to learn a rule and concept by name, use it in their own writing,
edit it in the writing of others, and observe it in professional writing.
Plan your own sequence within the year or two before students take
the SAT.

In the next chapter, you will learn more about the application of
grammatical knowledge to make sentences do just what the writer
wants them to do.

7 Rhetorical Grammar

In her seminal book, *Rhetorical Grammar: Grammatical Choices, Rhetorical Effects*, Martha Kolln speaks of understanding (what we already know about) grammar by bringing unconscious knowledge about grammar into the conscious level. By so doing, we can control the sentences we write, deliberately directing the reader's attention here or there, purposefully arranging words to deliver information, expanding phrases, constructing elements, and ordering information so that the reader's mind and the writer's mind meet each other most closely (4). The essence of rhetorical grammar, Kolln states, is to develop a mental tool kit consisting of grammatical terminology and concepts. The writer can do more than recognize and name the tools in the tool kit; the writer can select the proper tools for crafting the intended message with clarity, efficiency, and beauty of form.

Kolln explains that rhetorical grammar is a tool kit for the writer "offering . . . explanations of the rhetorical choices that are available" (x). In other words, the grammatical choices the writer makes—choices about placement of words, phrases, clauses; choices about punctuation; choices about how verbs are put to use—affect the way the writer's words will be received by the reader. Rhetorical grammar transcends the rules we need to know to fix up sentences so that they won't offend the reader's sensibilities about dangling modifiers and such; rhetorical grammar is the knowledge that puts the writer in control of focusing the reader's attention.

Though you may not be familiar with the term, *rhetorical grammar* is the ultimate reason for teaching grammar. Yet you won't find rhetorical grammar taught in most curricula. That is because we are so misguided about (1) what grammar instruction is good for and (2) the importance of correcting surface errors. I think we spend an inordinate amount of time fretting over surface errors at the expense of more substantial, rhetorical issues in a student's writing. When I make this assertion in my presentations to teachers, they usually become alarmed and indignant at the thought of an English teacher "not caring about" that which English teachers were put on the Earth to care deeply about: various stylistic choices that they consider errors—sentence fragments, comma splices, sentences that begin with coordinating conjunctions or that end with prepositions, split infinitives. It becomes hard for me to explain over the din of moral outrage that no, I don't think "anything goes," but, yes, I do think we need to "get over ourselves" sometimes and see the forest (meaning) for the trees (adherence to the rules of Standard English, rules that change and vary anyway). Instruction in rhetorical grammar is the transcendent step that allows grammar instruction to result in meaningful revision.

The nature of language is, always has been, and will continue to be such that some people will refuse to accept its evolving nature. Some people will place irrationally high value on mordant forms as the language evolves. They will attribute to those who say "With whom are you going?" even in casual conversation an intellectual, if not moral, superiority over those who say "Who are you going with?" For the purpose of progress, we shall return them to their deplorations and lamentations.

I believe there are two kinds of surface errors that concern us: those that interfere with meaning and those that compromise the credibility of the writer. The latter is going to depend on the sensibilities of the reader. Not everyone is equally disdainful of *less* for *fewer* or the sentence-ending preposition. Those transgressions do not interfere with meaning. There are two categories of errors that interfere with meaning: those that make the sentence incomprehensible or ambiguous and those that distract the reader and momentarily break the reader-writer contract. I call this the "flying gnat" problem: It's hard to concentrate on whatever you are doing if you have to swat away flying gnats.

Flying gnats include but are not limited to homonym misuse, egregious spelling errors, failure to capitalize proper nouns and the first word of a sentence, unintentional sentence fragments, and superfluous commas.

Speaking of rigidity, designating words in the English language as belonging rigidly to this or that part of speech out of context is wrongheaded. In the English language, words shift easily from one part of speech to another. The more knowledgeable we are about a subject, and the newer the semantic field, the freer we are with its words. *Partner*, *transition*, and *disconnect* are nouns that have functionally shifted so that we can *partner with someone on a project, transition to the new system*, and *cause a disconnect*. We can *lawyer up, outsource, input*, and *text message*. Things are *actionable* and *doable*. When we teach parts of speech with the dynamic living language in mind, students have a lot to contribute and reason to be interested.

Just as those interested in rhetorical grammar do not view words in isolation, neither do we view sentences in isolation. Rather, we view sentences as units of meaning that operate in harmony, in juxtaposition, and in a dependent relationship with their fellow sentences. A sentence has meaning to the reader only as *that* sentence relates to the meaning of the paragraph that it's in. Preposterously, we tell students that a sentence is a *complete thought*, and then we wonder why students have clause boundary problems!

Moving toward the goal of meaningful revision, we divide rhetorical grammar into four domains: concord, control of focus, liveliness, and detail. Each is a feature that improves communication through well-crafted text. Before we begin, let's establish that rhetorical grammar is most readily understood once we stop thinking that grammar is about single words having designated parts of speech and sentences being complete thoughts. The way that meaning is actually derived through language is more through phrases than through single words and through sentences as they operate in a paragraph.

Concord

By *concord*, I mean agreement, harmony, and cohesion. Concord is achieved through parallel structure, observation of the given/new principle, and meaningful repetition. (Undoubtedly, there are other contributors to concord, but these are the ones that I believe are most accessible to schoolchildren.)

Parallel structure is one of those terms that is hard to understand through definition but easy to recognize through example. Parallel structure is a language pattern in which the same grammatical structure is used within a sentence itself or within sentences in a paragraph, or even from paragraph to paragraph. Parallel structure creates rhythm and memorability (which is why it is used so heavily in oratory), evokes a sense of order, and gives written language a polished sense of craftsmanship. Students who can produce parallel structure are in position to elevate their writing immeasurably.

To teach parallel structure, three things are necessary:

1. Students must have an array of grammatical terminology so that they can call parallel elements by name: adjective/noun phrase, prepositional phrase, adverbial clause, adjectival clause, etc.

2. Students must develop the habit of recognizing parallel structure in text. They will start off being able to recognize just a few, the most obvious, examples. With practice, they will notice subtle instances of parallel structure. The best place to begin might be with poetry, then oratory, and then prose. A simple way for the novice to recognize parallel structure is to circle all

and's in text, looking for pairs of words, pairs of phrases, and pairs of clauses.

3. Students can then revise their own writing to include parallel structure for the same reasons the professionals do: for the rhetorical effect of orderliness and graceful craftsmanship.

On a more sophisticated rhetorical level, parallel structure can be expressed as chiasmus, an "inside out" form, as in *Ask not what your country can do for you, ask what you can do for your country*. This might not be the kind of sentence your students are likely to write, but many students are interested in knowing that words like *chiasmus* exist to designate rhetorical inversions.

Because of its rhythmic nature, parallel structure affects pace. When we want to slow down the pace and give each separate item in a series its own moment in the sun, we might want to employ *polysyndeton*, the insertion of a coordinating conjunction between each item in a series: *Lions and tigers and bears!*

The opposite of polysyndeton, *asyndeton*, speeds up the pace by eliminating the conjunction that would ordinarily signal the last item in the series: *Lions, tiger, bears!*

That is what parallel structure can do for us as a positive (what-to-do) model. In a negative (what-not-to-do) model, the lack of parallel structure is what we usually just condemn as *awkward*, a marginal comment that is famous for being unhelpful to students. A student writes: *Holden Caulfield left Pencey Prep because he was confused, depressed, and he failed all of his subjects except English*. There are various ways for the student to recraft this sentence if the student understands that it lacks parallelism: We have two subject complements (*confused, depressed*) and a subject-verb-direct object pattern as the third element. This sentence, a bit tricky, can be revised to read: *Holden Caulfield left Pencey Prep because he was confused, depressed, and unsuccessful in every subject except English*.

Concord is further achieved through something that rhetorical grammarians call the *given/new principle*. This principle posits that cohesion is achieved when sentences in text tend to present given (familiar, expected, thematic) information in the subject slot and new information in the predicate slot. By adhering to this principle, the writer controls the "information feedline" to the reader. (The three sentences you just read illustrate the given/new principle in action. Notice how the subject in the second sentence [*this principle*] refers to the direct object [*the given/new principle*] in the previous sentence. The third sentence opens by referring to a "given" idea, *this principle*.) Unless the writer purposely wishes to withhold information for a rhetorical effect, such as creating mystery, the reader should receive either new information or clarifying information in every sentence. The reader is entitled to read sentences that flow naturally from one to the next, lest information gaps between one sentence and the next create lapses in comprehension.

The given/new principle does not tie the writer down to writing sentence after sentence that begins with the subject word. In fact, doing just that is a hallmark of immature writing style and is exactly what we're trying to avoid when we advise students to *vary sentence structure*. Sentences that begin with prepositional phrases, adverbial structures, and subordinate clauses set the stage for the reader. However, when the reader's eyes do fall on the grammatical subject, that subject should be familiar territory within the text.

The *given* information in the subject slot can refer to the sentence that immediately precedes it or it can simply bring to mind the overall subject of the text. Many sentences begin with pronouns. Pronouns are always *given* (known, familiar) information, as they refer to a noun (phrase or clause). Many times, students give us pronouns that do *not* refer to anything we can name, creating that oh-so-well-known puzzlement ("Huh?") for the reader.

The problem in student writing is not so much that students don't have given information in the subject slot: The problem is that they have no new information in the predicate slot. A student might write like this:

> I think the most interesting character in *The Scarlet Letter* is Arthur Dimmesdale. He is the most intriguing character.

Or this:

> Roger Chillingworth changed from a man who was a learned physician who wanted to help people and cure diseases to a man who just was out for revenge. He went from being a doctor to being just revenge crazed.

The *new* information in the predicate slot is that which justifies the existence of the sentence, but you can see in the preceding student-written sentences that there is not sufficient (if any) new information to justify the existence of a sentence. Once I learned about the given/new principle, I began using it lavishly to comment on my students' writing. I often find myself writing *NNI*, an editorial abbreviation that to my students means "no new information."

We can think of the given (familiar/expected) information in the subject slot as "carryover" meaning. With your students, use colored pencils to set up a strong visual that represents the given/new principle.

Have students gently shade all new information, information that advances the reader's knowledge, in blue; have them shade all instances of carryover information in yellow; have them shade all transitional information in orange; and have them shade all summarizing information in green. The given/new pattern is what allows the writer to develop a piece that weaves meaning using two threads, one that continues the meaning (given) and the other that expands it (new).

Such color-coding leads to recognition of the importance of another rhetorical practice that supports cohesion: meaningful repetition. In *Meaning-Centered Grammar*, Craig Hancock describes a scenario in which a student is assigned a 1,500-word paper to write and is under the impression that repetition is a bad thing. Imagine that student's befuddlement, not having that much information available to deliver without any repetition! A student who believes that repetition is a thing to be avoided would not only be seriously daunted by almost any writing task, but that student would also be unaware of the rhetorical value of repetition as a strategy for achieving emphasis, unity, and rhythm (57). The student who is without knowledge about the value of repetition is likely to fail in two ways: sufficiency of information and cohesion (unity).

Hancock describes three *kinds* of repetition. The first is the given/new pattern. The second is called *lexical* repetition, the repetition of actual words—key words. I advise my students that they need to identify what their key words and phrases are going to be, based on the demands of the prompt. Then they need to think of those key words as nails, nails to be hammered into place at *various strategic points* in the piece. And the third kind of repetition comes through grammar: the repetition of grammatical structures, or parallel structure.

I teach my students that there are three *purposes* of repetition: unity, emphasis, and rhythm. If the key words are nailed into place at various strategic points, unity is achieved. The piece can't run too far away from its main idea (purpose) if the writer remembers to hammer down those key words. In music, this would be called the tonic, or keynote. Most pieces of music achieve a sense of unity and orderliness by ending on the tonic. Written compositions can end in this way as well. This leads to emphasis. Hancock speaks of tonic prominence: that the natural place of emphasis in a sentence comes at its end. As for rhythm, it is achieved through parallel structure (grammatical repetition). In African American church rhetoric, repetition that is rooted in the call-and-response motif connects the congregants to the preacher and establishes the keynote of the speech. In his speech at the 1984 Democratic

National Convention, Jesse Jackson used the refrain "They work every day" to spotlight the needs of America's working poor.

And so concord—agreement, unity, harmony—is achieved through the writer's conscious knowledge about how to use repetition and like structures to lead the reader gently from one idea to the next, much as a considerate trail guide might direct the steps of a new hiker over unfamiliar, sometimes rocky, sometimes slippery territory.

Focus

The careful writer makes grammatical choices that will have the rhetorical effect of directing the reader's attention to specific elements of text. Here I explain five techniques that allow the writer to deliberately control reader focus: tonic prominence (aka end focus), post-noun modification, commas, colons, and clefts/transformations.

In the previous segment, I discussed tonic prominence as a way of achieving strategic grammatical repetition through the given/new principle. Some grammarians or rhetoricians refer to the placement of focus-bearing information at the end of a clause as *end focus*. In a kind of sentence called a periodic sentence, the subject-verb nexus is delayed until the end of the sentence:

> Over the river and through the woods to grandmother's house <u>we go</u>.

A periodic sentence is demanding, but can be exciting to the reader:

> Alone and left to do household chores like folding laundry, dusting furniture, and polishing candlesticks, <u>Cinderella wept</u>.

Hancock gives this wonderful example of how tonic prominence (end focus) would affect the reader's perception in the following two sentences that might appear in a description of a student's performance:

> Her writing was always excellent, but usually late.

> Her writing was usually late, but always excellent. (60)

Needless to say, even though these two sentences contain identical words, the impact is quite different because of placement.

Another way to direct the reader's focus is to place modifiers somewhere other than in their usual position. Adjectives, modifiers of nouns, are generally placed in the pre-noun position:

> Yon Cassius has a lean and hungry look.

Or, as subject complements:

> Yon Cassius has a look that is lean and hungry.

But if I wanted to put those two adjectives under the lights, I might bring them out of their expected positions:

> Yon Cassius, *lean and hungry*, looks dangerous.

You'll note that two things happened when I repositioned the adjectives: The reader's focus shifted to the out-of-position adjectives, and the post-noun placement freed up a slot in the sentence for more information (*dangerous*).

Note that the post-noun adjectives are set off by commas. When the normal order of elements in English syntax is disrupted, we use commas to signal that condition. Commas are used to observe conventions (e.g., Chicago, Illinois; January 16, 2007); commas are used to prevent lapses in comprehension (e.g., *While Mother was cooking the dog ran away*); and commas are used to create waves of attention (Hancock 61). Read aloud to your students sentences having commas, exaggerating the pitch and volume, and you will see the rhetorical effects of commas and how they create emphasis on that which *precedes* them:

> Once upon a time, there lived a princess who, even though she was a princess, was sad because she felt that no one loved her.

Another useful tool is the colon. It is capable of turning an ordinary sentence into a dramatic one: That is its specialty. Novice writers generally think of the colon as having as its only use the introduction of a list. Intermediate writers understand that the colon allows them to say "in other words" or "namely." But skilled writers use the colon to speed up the pace and build tension before making an important point:

> Apathy is the source of all of our problems.

> All of our problems stem from one cause: apathy.

And the English language is capable of bringing in structures that don't really have meaning per se, but that have the function of pointing up a structure that follows them. A *cleft* is a division. We have what we call *it-clefts*, *what-clefts*, and *there-transformations*. Here's how these things work:

> I stole the cookie from the cookie jar.

Now look at how the emphasis falls on *I* when you use what is known as the *it-cleft*:

It was I who stole the cookie from the cookie jar.

Now look at how the *what-cleft* shifts emphasis:

What I stole from the cookie jar was not a cookie.

(Notice how cleft division here redirects the reader's attention to that which was stolen: the *not-a-cookie*.)

The *there-transformation* is what we call a sentence that begins with *There is/There are*. Almost always, the purpose of such a sentence is to introduce a new topic or to change the focus:

I found a cookie jar. *There were* two cookies stuck to the bottom of it.

And so we see that conscious rearrangement of elements within a sentence, the placement of commas, and the use of clefts and transformation allow us to cleverly manipulate the reader's attention.

Liveliness

We want our students to write crisp, concise, lively prose. For this rhetorical effect, we need to know when to use action verbs as opposed to *to be*; we need to prefer the active voice unless there is a reason to favor the passive voice; we need to have an animated being in the subject slot as much as possible; we need to avoid the overuse of nouns having noun-making suffixes (such as *-ity*, *-ment*, *-ation*). Instead of saying, "The personnel director made a recommendation that we should have a reduction of our expenditures," we can be more lively by simply saying, "The personnel director recommended that we reduce our spending." And we need to employ a healthy workforce consisting of verbals, as I just did by using *spending* rather than *expenditure*. Oh, it's not that *expenditure* is a naughty word; it's just that we shouldn't overdo it on the affixed words.

Everybody knows that action verbs work hard and get the job done. So let's let them do that. Hire a team of as many action verbs as possible. Pull them off the bench. Let them get into the game, doing what they do best: express *action*! Empower students with verb awareness, using authentic literature (and journalism and oratory) as a model. Don't stop with the finite verb: Point out how verbals punch up sentences and how active voice animates a sentence in a way that passive voice, though the right choice at times, may not.

Detail

We want our students to be able to write with rich detail: visuals, specifics, discerning information. Grammatically, information that provides detail can attach to the noun phrase or the verb phrase.

The noun phrase is wonderfully expandable. Look at how many modifiers can be added before and after the headword:

cottage (*This is our headword.*)

a cottage (*We precede the headword with a determiner.*)

a little cottage (*We add an adjective.*)

a little green cottage (*We add another adjective.*)

a little green country cottage (*We add a pre-noun noun that functions adjectivally.*)

a little light green cottage (*We add another adjective to modify the adjective "green."*)

a little light green cottage with wooden shutters (*We add a prepositional phrase that contains an adjective.*)

a little light green cottage with wooden shutters by the bay (*We add another prepositional phrase.*)

a little light green country cottage with wooden shutters overlooking the bay (*We add a participial phrase.*)

a little light green cottage with wooden shutters by the bay that I used to pass by every day on my way to work. . . . (*We've added an adjectival clause that has within it its own modifiers.*)

Verb phrases are expandable as well through adverbs, adverbial phrases, and adverbial clauses. Prepositional phrases are adverbial in function if they answer the questions that adverbs answer: *where? when? why? to what extent? in what manner?* Prepositional phrases are adjectival in function if they answer the questions that adjectives answer: *which one? what kind? how many?*

swim

swim in the lake (*We add a prepositional phrase.*)

swim like a professional in the crystal clear lake (*We add another prepositional phrase and adjectives modifying the object of one of the prepositional phrases.*)

swim in the lake when the weather turns warm in June (*We add an adverbial clause.*)

A TEACHER'S JOURNAL: APPOSITIVES

The class is immersed in study of Truman Capote's *In Cold Blood*. In preparation for the tenth-grade honors final, which is the New York State Regents exam, I give the students an essay assignment that will get them to explore the novel's themes. The exam asks the students to use a "critical lens" (or focus quote) as a prompt to explore texts; I'll be using the concept to gauge their ability to analyze the subtext, as well as to work on their writing skills. I give the students this quote:

In a dark time the eye begins to see.

Theodore Roethke

As I grade the essays, I jot down common errors and, more specifically, student sentences that require revision. When I hand back the essays, we perform a "postmortem," which means that, together, we dissect the sentences to achieve better clarity and varied perspective. The postmortem enables me to show the students relevant errors from their own work. I type up about ten sentences from their papers, and together we review and debate the problems, revising them individually and then, ultimately, as a class. When it comes to skills building, I find the students respond much better to their own writing than to sentences pulled out of an exercise book.

I know I need to address some grammatical subtleties, and this postmortem activity is the perfect vehicle. We go through the common errors: a splash of *affect/effect*, a dab of apostrophe, and a healthy portion of awkward phrasings—all common servings in the back-to-school kitchen. But one problem keeps popping up: Their sentences lack specific details and variety. I continually read sentences like, "Perry Smith is uneducated but wishes to be." Or, "Richard Hickock is not as brave as he pretends to be." Even, "Truman Capote's prose is full of vivid description." Although the sentences illuminate insight and are grammatically sound, they lack the kind of detail I know the students can produce with the proper tools.

Even the best writers, like Jeremy, with his keen insights and strong vocabulary, write with few specific adjectives and a bland formula. More specifically, he needs to learn the power of the appositive! I want to harness their desire to impress as well as their creativity while simultaneously introducing the concepts of detail and variety. For homework, I ask them to create a persona: "You can be anyone you want: an astronaut who placed the flag on Pluto, a famous musician with a fear of performing, an English teacher with bad ties and a temper like a tempest. Have fun with this! Be creative and give me truckloads of descriptive adjectives." I keep the assignment pretty open. Just a few sentences packed with specific adjectives, encouraging them to have a little fun with it. And I know they will.

The next day they pour in, glowing with the murmurs of imaginative prowess. Eagerly sharing their ideas, they don't wait for the bell. Really. They're talking about the assignment, trying to get my ear. Before I even mention my objective, we go around the room sharing our new monikers. Doug is a six-foot-seven Canadian lumberjack known for his delicate lacework and his thriving ant farm. Khine is an alien named Lanethea from the planet Voltairius, Danny an iguana salesman from Kansas with chronic back trouble and a fascination with feet, Shira a Pulitzer Prize–winning author known for her sharp commentary on global warming as it relates to romantic relationships. They have nailed the exercise and are ready for the next step.

I tell them that writers begin most of their sentences with the subject, and that one of the best ways to add flare and variety to sentences is to employ the appositive. On the board, I write: *John is a cool guy. Hamlet is an icon of literature. Barry Bonds will have a big game tonight*. I am being abstract, hoping they will slowly construct the concept for themselves. Next to the sentences, I write: <u>*Appositive*</u>—*a renamer giving additional noun information; an appositive can expand the meaning of a noun or noun phrase. Essentially, appositives identify, explain, or otherwise supplement the meaning of nouns or noun phrases*. Of course, after copying this into their notebooks, the students want to know when we are getting back to the personas. Using colored markers, I turn to the board and write: *John,* **my neighbor**, *is a cool guy. Hamlet,* **the contemplative tragic hero of Shakespeare's masterpiece**, *is an icon of literature. Barry Bonds,* **the homerun machine**, *will have a big game tonight*. There is a hum in the room. Ryan calls out, "I get it! The appositive tells us more about the person!" "Yes," I say. "And Truman Capote uses them too." On the board, I write: *"Mrs. Clutter,* **a near-sighted woman**, *removed her rimless glasses and pressed her eyes" (26). "Instead, she had met and married Herb,* **a college classmate of her oldest brother**, *Glenn . . ." (26)*. Emilio, shy but unable to hold back his epiphany, mutters, "It really does add clarity." "That's right!" I say, repeating his quiet comment, "And now it's your turn to give it a try."

On the board I write: *Using the persona you prepared for class, create at least three sentences using an appositive*. The room is silent and busy. Not only are students learning a new concept, but they are having a good time doing it. Some students do have questions, especially about using commas to identify the appositive, but after quickly circling the room, I find that they're all on their way with confidence and enthusiasm. We share ideas and have a good laugh. Then I move on to using appositives to vary sentence structure.

On the board, I write: *My neighbor, John, is a cool guy.* Emily, perceptive and quick, always the first with a question, throws her hand in the air. "Do you really need the commas? Is that still an appositive?" I explain that the commas aren't always necessary. The writer decides whether the reader needs commas around the appositive to discern meaning. And that, yes, it's still an appositive. I want to add depth to the lesson as well as place it in the context of their writing for analysis.

With about fifteen minutes left, I reveal the final layers of the concept. On the board, I write: *Using either a character or the author of one of your summer reading texts, write three sentences that give the specific details before the name. Ex. "Quirky, compassionate, and courageous, Pi Patel is the protagonist of the novel <u>Life of Pi</u>."* The students are already experts, scribbling away without realizing they are exploring higher-level writing.

With the final few minutes, I leave the names behind and illuminate how to use an appositive for a noun or noun phrase that isn't a person. I ask the students to invite their persona to an event, such as a historical event, party, or sporting event. Without further prompting, students are running with the idea. Julien calls to Alissa, "Hey, wanna come to my seventies dance party?" Aaron, raising his hand but unable to hold back, yelps, "I'm going to colonize Pluto and beyond! And we're going to grow plants that make music!" They are rolling, I am thrilled, and we are all enjoying a meaningful, memorable engagement with grammar.

For homework, I ask students to write a short paragraph full of appositives, specifically focusing on describing their events and varying how they open the sentences.

Not wanting to overcook the concept, or take too much time, I visit the homework briefly the next day. I know students will want to share (even take the whole period if they can), but I want to model the concept for them first to avoid any confusion and move things along. On the board, I write the following three sentences: *The show had an unexpected twist—a guest appearance by Jay-Z. To get an A in Mr. Oliva's class, you must incorporate the essentials of quality writing: focus, organization, conventions and creativity. <u>In Cold Blood</u>, a novel set in the small town of Holcomb, Kansas, evokes empathy from even the coldest heart.* I explain that normally we wouldn't overwhelm a paragraph with appositives, just place them here and there for variety. I also highlight the use of the dash and the colon in the examples and encourage students to use this punctuation too.

The students' examples prove that the concept has been successfully incorporated, and the students' enthusiasm tells me they will use the appositive in the future. For extra incentive, I add, "Two points added to any essay that successfully utilizes the appositive for details and variety! Don't overdo it!"

Conclusion

If the problem with teaching grammar is the lack of transfer and application from the lesson to students' academic and personal writing, teaching grammar for rhetorical effects is the solution. Rhetorical grammar opens students' minds to their own control of the English language, enabling them to create sentences that are interesting, varied, balanced, clear, and beautiful. After all the huffing and puffing we've done getting students to understand and be able to speak about grammar, rhetorical grammar feels like the promised land we've been climbing up to.

In the next and final chapter, I talk about how to put all of this information about rhetorical grammar together in a scope and sequence that gets the job done in a developmentally appropriate manner.

8 Scope and Sequence

- "Where do we begin?"
- "We've been teaching traditional grammar, with no success. What we teach is just not transferred to the students' writing. How would we transition into a new kind of grammar instruction?"
- "How would we get everyone on board?"
- "What's the best grade to start grammar instruction?"

These are the questions I invariably hear when I give workshops in linguistic grammar to teachers and English supervisors. They're interested. They want to learn. They see how linguistic grammar can be integrated with literature and writing instruction. They get how grammar can be taught in an exciting, brain-compatible way. But they don't know how to organize the whole thing. Teachers want a scope and sequence.

If you have a scope and sequence, you don't feel so much like you are groping around in the dark to find what the students have at least been exposed to. Grammar learning is highly recursive in nature, and we can expect to have to go over concepts and terminology that students have supposedly learned before; with a scope and sequence, we can at least know what they *haven't* been exposed to. Of course, in our mobile society, we need to be prepared for a good number of students who come to us from other districts. But at least, with a scope and sequence in place, we can provide some background for entering students that will bring them up to speed.

Most K–12 school districts do have a curriculum guide that lays out what should be taught and when (scope and sequence). That document, however, is often all but useless when it comes to discovering what students actually know and need to know at given grade levels. This is because traditional grammar, though taught, doesn't get learned, for all intents and purposes. So what I present in this chapter is a suggested scope and sequence for grammar instruction that has the following characteristics:

1. It integrates grammar instruction with the other language arts: literature, writing, oratory and rhetoric, oral communications in various contexts.

2. It spans grades 4–11 in four segments: grades 4–5, 6–7, 8–9, and 10–11. Teachers in grades K–3 usually attend to writing complete sentences, and I've addressed how I think this is best

done in the early primary grades; I don't think actual grammatical terminology is necessary at this point in a child's education.

3. It suggests pedagogy that is supported by research in brain-compatible learning, specifically, the research of Eric Jensen and of Renate and Geoffrey Caine and colleagues. It trusts the natural human proclivity to love language play, to find patterns, to be sociable, and to learn through visuals and manipulatives.

4. Though it leads to understandings of the conventions of Standard Written English, it eschews the notion of "one right and true" way of speaking English. In teaching the conventions of SWE, this scope and sequence is respectful of the diversity of the English-speaking world. It relies on the principle that language *changes* and language *varies*.

5. In explaining how to execute the scope and sequence, I've divided each of the five grade-level ranges into four parts:

    a. Content and Application

    b. Suggested Pedagogy

    c. Terminology

    d. Summary

A Scope and Sequence for Grammar Instruction

Objective: Students should be able to understand and talk about the English language in a way that allows them to make effective rhetorical choices.

In accordance with research endorsed by NCTE (http://www.ncte.org/collections/grammar), teachers should rely on the following to teach grammar:

1. Authentic literature

2. Student-generated writing

3. Visuals and manipulatives: colors, blocks that can be moved to represent different sentence parts, picture cards, etc.

4. The students' natural language sense, which comprises an astonishing amount of prior knowledge

5. Active learning pedagogy: socializing, dramatics, humor, wordplay, creative and critical thinking, use of prior knowledge, pattern-finding

6. The principle that language *changes* and language *varies*. Language changes and varies in accordance with the communicative context.

If you'd like more information on NCTE's suggestions for grammar instruction, you may refer to "Some Questions and Answers about Grammar" at http://www.ncte.org/about/over/positions/category/gram/107646.htm.

Grades K–3

Students do compose in the early grades of elementary school. Therefore, they need to know what a sentence is, that there are different kinds of sentences, and that punctuation is used in writing as something that writers do to help the reader understand when to pause, when to stop and rest, and how to make your voice (aloud or in your head) transform the written language into the spoken language.

Content and Application

The goal is to have students recognize and be able to apply the following:

- *Capital letters*: Capital letters, as opposed to lowercase letters, signal proper nouns and sentence beginnings.
- *Features of written language*: Written language has features that oral language does not have, and vice versa.
- *The beginning and end of a sentence*: These are signaled by two conventions: capital letters begin sentences, and punctuation ends them.
- *Elaboration of a basic sentence*: Once we write a sentence, we can enrich that sentence by adding descriptive information.
- *Nouns*: At this primary stage, the following simplified "definition" of a noun will do fine: "If you can put the word *the* in front of a word, then that word is called a noun."
- *Word endings*: Words in English can sometimes have endings. These endings change something about the word or allow the word to be used in a certain way.

Suggested Pedagogy

- The major pedagogy I would suggest for children in these early years is simple: *Read aloud, read aloud, read aloud*. When children hear what written English sounds like, they are getting a sense of the cadence of an English sentence. It is that cadence, more than all the grammar lessons in the world, that will help them understand clause boundaries.
- Provide an environment that is visually print-rich.
- Include a variety of genre in the child's exposure to written language. Story text, wonderful as it is, is not the whole story. Chil-

dren need to hear and see written language in mathematics, social studies, and science as well.

- Help students recognize three kinds of sentences: statements, questions, and commands.

- Help students recognize that there are times, such as in a list, when a writer chooses to use fragments (and that fragments are not always bad).

Terminology

The following explanations are not orthodox glossary definitions. Rather, they set forth age-appropriate understandings that move the child toward fuller understandings later on, just as games like Scrabble for Juniors is the age-appropriate version of the more sophisticated game.

- *Sentence*: A group of words that is either a statement, a question, or a command (see below)

- *Statement*: A sentence that gives information (tells you something); you can put the words *It is true that* . . . in front of a statement

- *Question*: A sentence that asks for information

- *Command*: A sentence that gives an order; you can say "please" before this kind of sentence

- *Fragment*: Part of a sentence; a fragment is a group of words that means something, but it doesn't sound quite like a sentence

- *Capital letter*: Used to begin sentences and to give a person's name or the name of a place on a map or calendar

- *Lowercase letter*: All other letters that are not capital letters

- *Period*: Marks the end of a statement or command

- *Question mark*: Marks the end of a question

- *Exclamation point*: Marks the end of a statement or command

- *Comma*: A mark that says "Pause"

- *Quotation marks*: Marks that take the words right out of the speaker's mouth; marks that name a title of a poem or story

- *Paragraph*: A group of sentences that go together as a group

In the course of reading, children will encounter many marks of punctuation, especially commas and quotation marks. They can certainly learn at this point that a comma asks the reader to pause and that quotation marks take the words right out of someone's mouth or name a title.

Summary

In these primary grades, the student's chief job is to learn to understand that although written language is another way of receiving and expressing information, written language and spoken language have significant differences. The most durable and useful thing that young children can learn—and that will lead to receptivity to grammar instruction—is that the English sentence falls on the ear in certain rhythms. These rhythms will later be demarcated as phrases, clauses, and sentences.

Grades 4–5 5×4

Content and Application

If students come to us in the fourth grade having a pattern-based sense of what the written English language sounds like in various genres, they will be in position to understand that a sentence is divisible into subject and predicate, and that the subject and predicate, in turn, can often be further divided into units called phrases. Teaching phrases means teaching the relationship between part and whole. Therefore, the teaching of phrases is analogous to the teaching of parts and wholes in other subjects. At this level, students would be learning about other parts, such as fractions, states in the union, molecules, syllables, chapters, etc. It is an important concept for children to understand that a *component* differs from a *miniature*. I like to use the example of a snow globe to explain how a miniature is different from a component.

At this level, students can begin to form an understanding of verbs and how verbs morph to indicate the time zone of their actions: tense. At this point, all students need to know is that a *verb* is a word that lives in the predicate and tells you what the subject is doing or being. An easy way to get the verb to tell you where it is is simply to turn the sentence into a negative (or vice versa, for a sentence that is already in the negative). For example, to find the verb in *Goldilocks fell asleep in the bed that was just the right size*, we find two verbs by making the sentence negative: *Goldilocks did not fall asleep in the bed that was not just right*. Notice how the negative-making words land right on the verbs like some kind of verb-seeking missile.

To introduce tense, we just need to ask (of sentences in authentic literature): Is this something that is happening now, or did this happen in the past? Through this kind of questioning, we can introduce the terms *present tense* and *past tense*. Students can be directed to notice that the *-ed* ending often creates the past tense; however, since our most common verbs are irregular, students also need to notice that there are countless other ways for a verb to tell you that it "happened in the past." (At this point, we needn't fret about what we may have learned about progressive or perfect tenses. Just divide everything into present or past. Don't even worry about verbs that express the future. In the sentence *We will see . . .*, the word *see* is in the present tense; in *I have seen . . .*, the verb can be said to refer to the past. Further information about the time zones of verbs can wait until later.)

Suggested Pedagogy

We want students to develop a feel for the two-part nature of an English sentence. For this to happen, we need to continue to rely on the aural and visual modeling that is accomplished through reading aloud and providing a print-rich environment. The traditional way of marking off subject and predicate is to underline the subject once, the predicate twice. This tradition still serves, but students will find it more interesting if we call on the senses and body as learning modalities.

- Use color codes for subject and predicate.
- For subject-verb recognition, substitute a pronoun for the subject to discover the subject-predicate border.
- Divide the class into two halves, each to read the subject and predicate, respectively, of sentences having similar patterns.
- Use manipulatives such as blocks (preferably color-coded), LEGOs, and Reading Rods.
- Mix and match sentence parts. Use strips of paper to write the sentences that form a familiar story. Cut the sentences in half, giving some students subjects and others the corresponding predicates. Turn the students loose to find their "partners." Then have a group reading of the story, with the students holding their sentence parts in front of them as they read.
- Use flash cards of animals and items. Call these flash cards "noun cards." Use them to show that expanded noun phrases, though they contain several words and can be quite elaborate, have the same referent: *The cow* is the same referent as *the brown and white cow wearing a cowbell*.

(New) Terminology

Remember that these, like the set of terms for K–3, are "juniorized" definitions that *move toward* the fuller explanations in the glossary.

> *Subject*: The words that tell you who or what the sentence is about
>
> *Predicate*: The words that give you news about the subject: What is the subject doing or being?

Phrase: Words that stick together within the subject or within the predicate; a phrase does not make a complete sentence

Noun phrase: A noun plus the words (or other phrases) that belong with it

Verb: A word that tells you what the subject is doing or being

Present tense: The form of the verb that we use when the action or being is habitual (happening on a regular basis)

Past tense: The form of the verb that we use when the action or being happened in the past (e.g., yesterday)

Progressive form: The *-ing* form of a verb; every single verb in the English language can be made into this form; the progressive form is used with forms of *be* as the auxiliary

Perfect form: The form of the verb that is used with forms of *have* as the auxiliary

Perfect progressive form: The form of the verb that is used with both the *have* and the *be* auxiliaries

Regular verb: A verb that forms its past tense and participle simply by adding the *-ed* ending

Irregular verb: A verb whose past tense and past participle are not formed by adding *-ed* (*go/went/gone*; *write/wrote/written*); in some cases, there is no change (*hit/hit/hit*; *put/put/put*; *set/set/set*)

Summary

In the fourth and fifth grades, students will come to understand that a sentence is a two-part thing, and that these two parts are called the subject and the predicate. The subject tells who or what the sentence is about; the predicate tells what the subject is doing or being in the sentence. The predicate always has a verb, which is the "engine" of the sentence. The verb reveals itself when you try to make a sentence negative (or when you try to do the reverse with a sentence that already is negative).

Students at this level will also understand that within the sentence we can find words that "stick together," and that words that stick together are called phrases. If a group of words sticks together and does *not* form a complete sentence, then we call that group of words a phrase. (Use the trick of putting the words *It is true that* . . . before a group of words to test whether it is a complete sentence.) If you can put *the* in front of that phrase, then we call it a noun phrase. It's important that students think of noun phrases as phrases, because the noun phrase functions as a unit within the sentence. It is the noun phrase, and not the lone noun, for example, that is "replaced" by a pronoun. It is the noun phrase, and not the lone noun, that names the referent.

Students will learn to use the preceding terminology to talk with their teachers and one another about syntax.

Grades 6–7

According to this scope and sequence, by the time students in this district reach the early middle school years, they are prepared to learn how to make their sentences more interesting through expansions of phrases, compounds, and varied placement of grammatical elements.

Content and Application

Students will learn to recognize **complete sentences** in order to accomplish the following:

- Writing complete sentences rather than fragments, run-ons, or comma splices
- Expanding subjects and predicates
- Locating phrases within the sentence

Students will learn to recognize **prepositional phrases** in order to accomplish the following:

- Varying sentence structure by beginning some sentences with introductory prepositional phrases
- Enriching sentences by using prepositional phrases to provide information about time and place
- Establishing subject-verb agreement by disregarding intervening prepositional phrases
- Recognizing prepositional phrases as functioning either adverbially or adjectivally. They function adverbially when they answer the questions that adverbs answer (*where? when? why? to what extent? in what manner?*); they function adjectivally when they answer the questions that adjectives answer (*which one? what kind? how many?*).

Students will learn to recognize **auxiliary verbs**, including **modal auxiliaries**, in order to accomplish the following:

- Creating sentences that express action in more than one time zone
- Using verb formations to express subtleties of action
- Maintaining consistency of verb tense

Students will learn to recognize **participles**, as they form the **perfect and progressive tenses** (aka *aspects*).

Suggested Pedagogy

For sentence completeness:

- Teach that a group of words is a complete (declarative) sentence when you can attach a "tag question" to it.

- Use simple sentences and, later, compound sentences extracted from the literature the students are already reading; notice, name, and apply punctuation for compound sentences.

- Have students attach tag questions on sticky notes to their own writings.

For prepositional phrases:

- To teach the array of prepositions, use the visual, such as a big rock, to serve as the object of various prepositions in order to teach the array of prepositions: *Somewhere _____ the rainbow.*

- Show students *Highlights* magazine's Hidden Pictures drawings: In telling where they find the hidden items, students will be speaking in prepositional phrases.

- Involve students in The Squirrel and the Post-it notes: Where did the squirrel hide his acorns?

(Answers will form prepositional phrases that function adverbially because they tell "where.")

For sentence expansion:

- Using a T-chart, add modifiers to the subject slot and the predicate slot.

- Have students create compound sentences and punctuate compound sentences.

(New) Terminology

Here is a list of new terminology. At this point in their learning, if students have been led through the scope and sequence, they can handle the definitions, which are fully developed in the glossary.

Phrase

Clause

Independent clause

Tag question

Sentences classified by purpose: declarative, exclamatory, interrogative, imperative

Simple sentence

Compound sentence
Compound elements
Parallel structure
Coordinating conjunction
Joined sentences
Dependent (aka subordinate) clause
Subject
Pronoun
Auxiliary
Modal auxiliary
"Do" support
Preposition
Object of a preposition
Prepositional phrase
Form-class words
Structure-class words

Summary

In the sixth and seventh grades, students will develop patterns of thinking about language that enable them to *clearly* understand how to recognize and produce complete sentences (simple and compound). They will also learn how to punctuate a compound sentence, making effective choices as to how to join independent clauses. Students will achieve this basic and crucial awareness by using the tag question technique against the sentences that appear in the literature they read and the sentences they and their peers write in the course of the writing process.

They will also understand how prepositional phrase knowledge can help them add dimension to their sentences, vary their sentence beginnings, and establish subject-verb agreement by recognizing the noun headword, disregarding intervening modifiers. Students will achieve this by noticing and naming prepositional phrases (and how they are placed) in the sentences that appear in the literature they read and the sentences they and their peers write in the course of the writing process.

Students will learn to use the preceding terminology to talk with their teachers and one another about syntax.

Grades 8–9

Content and Application

It is at this point that students who have the previous information under their belts can really dip into complex structures. It is now that they can incorporate subordinating elements into their sentences. Further, they can learn to use modifiers in sophisticated ways, controlling the focus and rhythm of their syntax.

Students will learn to recognize **complex sentences** in order to accomplish the following:

- Writing (complex) sentences to bring together information in which one idea is subordinate to another
- Understanding the cues in sentences that explain the relationship of main and subordinate ideas
- Making decisions about the placement and punctuation of main and subordinate clauses

Students will learn to recognize structures that join subordinate clauses to main clauses (**relative pronouns, subordinating conjunctions**).

Students will learn to recognize **conjunctive adverbs**, which join main clauses (i.e., compound sentences).

Students will learn to recognize **verb phrases** and **tenses** in order to accomplish the following:

- Using more than one verb tense in a sentence to express different "time zones"
- Using the proper Standard English form of irregular verbs
- Understanding the difference between, and the rules that govern, action and linking verbs

Students will learn to recognize **adjectives** and **adverbs** as **modifiers** in order to accomplish the following:

- Knowing how to punctuate modifiers within a sentence (when to use and when not to use commas)
- Knowing whether to form and use an adverb or an adjective
- Knowing when to use pre- and post-noun modifiers
- Creating adverbials and adjectival phrases and clauses

Students will learn how to use the **semicolon** and the **colon** and how to **expand the noun phrase**.

Knowledge of the preceding information will enable students not only to construct but also to edit sentences that have correct agreement and placement of structures to convey a clear message.

Suggested Pedagogy

- Use model sentences from the literature that is already part of the curriculum.
- Use sentences from students' writing produced in the course of the writing process.

(New) Terminology

Here are the new terminology and expansions of terms previously learned:

Complex sentence: A sentence that consists of a main clause and a dependent (aka subordinate) clause. If the main clause comes first, no comma is needed to separate it from the dependent adverbial clause. But if the dependent clause comes first, a comma is needed to separate it from the independent clause.

Subordinating conjunction: A word or phrase that introduces (links) a dependent adverbial clause to a main clause.

Relative pronoun: A word that introduces a relative clause (i.e., adjectival clause). Examples of relative pronouns are *who*, *which*, *that*, *whoever*, *whichever*, etc.

Conjunctive adverb: A word used with a semicolon to connect coordinate sentences (e.g., *however*, *moreover*, *so*).

Adverb, adverbial: An adverb answers one of these questions: *when? where? why? to what extent? in what manner?* In addition to adverbs themselves, phrases and clauses that answer these questions within a sentence are called *adverbials*.

Adjective, adjectival: An adjective answers this question: *what kind?* If you can insert a word into the following frame, then the word is an adjective: *The _____ truck is very _____.* Phrases and clauses that answer these questions within a sentence are called *adjectivals*. To determine whether a word is an adverb or adjective, see if you can put *very* in front of it. If you can, then the word is an adverb or an adjective.

Determiner: A determiner signals a noun. When you see a determiner, you know that you are at the beginning of a noun phrase. Definite and indefinite articles (*the*, *a*, *an*) function as determiners, as do demonstrative pronouns (*this*, *that*, *these*, *those*), numbers that precede nouns, and possessive pronouns (*my*, *our*, *its*, *his*, *her*, *their*) and nouns (*Pete's*, *my mother's*).

Summary

By the end of ninth grade, then, students should be able to compose very complex syntax with expanded noun and verb phrases. They should be able to apply the rules of Standard English to establish agreement and create clarity in a sentence that has a sophisticated structure. And they should be able to make conscious, well-informed decisions about when to use action verbs and when to use linking verbs.

Grades 10–11

Students who have come this far in our scope and sequence are positioned to talk in sophisticated ways about the language they produce and receive. They are in position to have enormous control over what they say and how they say it to achieve clarity, style, conciseness, elaboration, and voice.

Content and Application

Students should be able to identify and effectively use the following:

- Verbals: Use of verbals (participles, gerunds, infinitives) to strengthen the language of sentences
- Stylistic fragments: Deliberate use of fragments to establish informal tone, when appropriate
- Parallel structure: Parallel structure to grace sentences with orderliness and rhythm
- Appositives: Appositives to strengthen sentences with additional noun information that renames a key noun in the sentence
- Post-noun modifiers: Post-noun modifiers to give modifiers special attention and to give prose a poetic sound
- Absolute phrases: Absolute phrases to give sentences a carefully crafted, polished sound
- Idioms: Knowledge of idioms, particularly with verbs (e.g., concerned *with*, rather than concerned *on*), satisfies standardized test questions and eliminates regional tendencies that can be stigmatized in formal writing and speech.
- Comparisons: Standardized tests often have questions that require recognition of fully formed wording in comparisons (e.g., *The Hudson River is more scenic than any <u>other</u> river in America; Sara is the <u>more</u> beautiful of the two Johnson girls; The characters in Shakespeare's tragedies are more complex than <u>those</u> of the comedies*).
- Pronoun case, number, reference: The called-for pronoun case (subjective, objective, possessive) must be applied in formal written English; pronoun case and pronoun-referent agreement in gender and number is a common kind of question on standardized tests.

Suggested Pedagogy

- Use model sentences from the literature that is already part of the curriculum.
- Use sentences from students' writing produced in the course of the writing process.

Terminology

Verbals

Stylistic fragments

Parallel structure

Appositive

Post-noun modifier

Idiom

Summary

By the end of the eleventh grade, students will be able to construct sentences that show literary and stylistic flair. They will also be able to answer the questions about usage that appear on the writing sections of the PSAT, SAT, and ACT tests. These questions do not require that the students name or apply specific grammatical labels. Rather, they require students to select the version of a sentence that best comports with Standard Written English.

Can I Get There from Here?

This scope and sequence may make sense to you but leave you saying, "Well, that would be great, but what do I do with my students while I'm waiting for such a scope and sequence to be established, and for students to come through the grades knowing this amount of grammar"? You can't wait for a scope and sequence to ripple on up to where you are. That would take years. You want to start now.

Obviously, the further down the grade levels you teach, the less information you would have to compress to bring students up to speed. If you teach the upper grades, it's reasonable to assume you may have to pick and choose concepts, or you may have to spend more time on grammar than you will have to do once the scope and sequence is established. While doing so, however, you'll be honing your grammar teaching skills, and you'll reap the rewards of finally being able to speak "the language of the language" to discuss reading, writing, and speaking.

Taxonomy and Terminology

Grammar Alive! A Guide for Teachers (Haussamen) has a glossary whose terms and definitions I've used here. I've organized the terms into twelve clusters:

- Phrases
- Sentences
- Language
- Structure of words
- Conjunctions
- Clause boundary errors
- Agreement conditions
- Nominals
- Pronouns
- Modifiers
- Adjectives
- Verbs

Much of grammar instruction involves defining terms and then identifying them. Many grammar instructors stop right there, as though learning grammar were similar to bird-watching ("Oh, look, I see an adjective!"). Grammar learning has to be about more than defining and identifying. It has to be about using grammatical terminology to have purposeful conversation and understandings about language and what it can do.

Learning terminology in clusters makes sense. If you were to take a cooking class, you would learn about the different kinds of kitchen tools in useful categories: those that cut, those that flatten, those that mix, etc.

Cluster I: Phrases

It is essential that students understand that phrases function as a unit of meaning. English sentences work by having different kinds of phrases perform different kinds of functions. Some phrases are movable without altering meaning; others are not movable. Usage matters; dangling modifiers and ambiguous reference can occur when phrases are moved too far away from whatever it is they are supposed to modify. The beauty of language is enhanced when we arrange phrases in similar ways, creating parallel structure. The important thing to remember about a phrase is that a phrase is not a clause, because a phrase does not have both a subject and a predicate. A phrase is usually part of either the subject or the predicate of a clause; it can also be a modifier of the sentence as a whole.

Phrase: A word or group of words that functions as a unit in the sentence and is not a clause. *The boy* is a noun phrase. *The boy with the blue shirt* is a noun phrase that includes a prepositional phrase modifying the noun *boy*. *The boy who is mowing the lawn* is a noun phrase that includes an adjective clause modifying the noun *boy*. See also **Noun phrase; Verb phrase; Preposition; Absolute phrase.**

Preposition: A structure-class word that combines with a nominal (the object of the preposition) to form a prepositional phrase, which functions adjectivally or adverbially, as in <u>On Tuesday</u>, *the circus came <u>to town</u>*.

Verb phrase (verb + its modifiers): A verb together with its auxiliaries, modifiers, and complements. The predicate of the sentence is a verb phrase, as in *He <u>left all his belongings, including his guitar, in the house</u>*. The term is sometimes used more narrowly to refer to just the main verb and its auxiliaries. See also **Main verb string.**

Phrasal verb: A verb consisting of a verb plus a particle, as in We <u>looked up</u> the words.

Absolute phrase: A noun phrase with one modifier, often a participial phrase, following the noun headword. An absolute phrase can explain a cause or condition, as in *<u>The temperature having dropped suddenly</u>, we decided to build a fire in the fireplace*, or it can add a detail or a point of focus, as in *The children rushed out the schoolhouse door, <u>their voices filling the playground with shouts of freedom</u>*.

Gerund phrase: A gerund together with all of its complements and modifiers, as in *<u>Playing the piano</u> is relaxing*.

Participial phrase: A present or past participle together with its complements and/or modifiers: *<u>Balancing their pizza and their drinks in their hands</u>, the kids left the room*.

Cluster II: Clauses and Sentences

Just as the union of sperm and egg creates the zygote, the union of subject and verb creates the clause. If the clause can stand alone on its own two feet, then we call it an independent clause. An independent clause is a sentence. A clause with some kind of conjunction attached to it is, like a truck with a hitch, subordinate or dependent. A subordinate clause (aka dependent clause) is not allowed to stand alone as a sentence, but must be hitched up to an independent clause.

Clause: A sequence of words that includes a subject and a predicate:

> **Independent clause:** The main clause of a sentence, one that can stand on its own: *The house that used to look run down is now painted a bright blue.*
>
> **Dependent clause (subordinate clause):** A clause that fills a role in a sentence (such as adverbial, adjectival, or nominal) and that cannot stand independently as a sentence: *He climbed until he was exhausted* (adverbial clause); *I wonder where I put my keys* (nominal clause functioning as direct object); *the house that used to look run down is now painted a bright blue* (adjectival, or relative clause).
>
> **Relative clause:** A clause introduced by a relative pronoun (*who, which, that*) or a relative adverb (*when, where, why*) that generally functions as an adjectival, as in *The book that you wanted has arrived; The area where I live is densely populated.* The *which* clause sometimes functions as a sentence modifier: *John bought a gas-guzzler, which surprised me.*

Simple sentence: A sentence consisting of a single independent clause, as in *Computers can be frustrating.*

Compound sentence: A sentence consisting of two or more independent, or main, clauses, as in *Computers are frustrating sometimes, but we all use them anyway.*

Complex sentence: A sentence consisting of one independent, or main, clause and at least one dependent clause, as in *Computers are frustrating when they don't work.*

Compound-complex sentence: A sentence consisting of two or more independent clauses and at least one dependent clause, as in *Computers are frustrating when they don't work, but we all use them anyway.*

Declarative sentence: A sentence in the form of a statement (in contrast to a command, a question, or an exclamation): *April showers bring May flowers.*

Exclamatory sentence: A sentence that expresses excitement or emotion. It may include a shift in word order and is usually punctuated with an exclamation point, as in *What a beautiful day we're having!*

Imperative sentence: A sentence in the form of a direction or a command; the subject, *you*, is usually deleted, as in *Turn left at the light; Come here; Be quiet.*

Interrogative sentence: A sentence in the form of a question (in contrast to a statement, exclamation, or command): *When are we leaving?*

Subject: The opening position in the basic structure of a sentence, filled by a noun phrase or other nominal that functions as the topic of the sentence, as in *This old upright piano still sounds beautiful.*

Predicate: One of the two principal parts of the sentence, it's the comment made about the subject. The predicate includes the verb together with its complements and modifiers: *The building finally collapsed after years of decay.*

Purpose: The chief reason for a sentence: declarative, interrogative, exclamatory, imperative.

Structure: The fundamental organization of a sentence: simple, compound, complex, compound-complex.

Verb Patterns:

    Linking verb: A verb that links the complement to the sentence subject, as in *The chicken is tasty; The salad looks delicious; The chef just became my husband.*

    Intransitive verb: A verb that requires no complement, although it may take an adverbial modifier: *Denzel's parents arrived at the airport.*

    Transitive verb: A verb that requires a direct object as its complement to be complete, as in *He drove the car.* Many verbs can be either transitive or intransitive: *Charles drove.* Most transitive verbs can be made passive: *The car was driven by Charles.*

Complement: A structure that completes the predicate, such as a direct object (*She planted roses*), indirect object (*He gave her a kiss*), subject complement (*He became sleepy*), and object complement (*She named him Theodore*).

Subject Complement: The nominal or adjectival that follows a linking verb and renames or modifies the sentence subject: *Charlestown, South Carolina, is a beautiful city.*

    Predicate Adjective: The adjective that functions as a subject complement following a linking verb, as in *He became sleepy.* Note that the adjective *sleepy* describes (modifies) the subject *he.*

    Predicate Nominative: The noun or nominal that functions as a subject complement: *She became an engineer.*

Direct object: A noun phase or other nominal structure that names the goal or receiver of the action of the verb, as in *Phil bought a used motorcycle; I enjoy watching basketball; I hope that it doesn't rain tomorrow.*

Indirect object: The noun phrase naming the recipient of the direct object. Indirect objects can be shifted into prepositional phrases with *to* or *for*, as in *Samantha gave her father a ticket; Samantha gave a ticket to her father.*

Object complement: A word or phrase in the predicate that completes the idea of the verb and modifies or renames the direct object: *I found the play exciting; We consider Rose Marie a good friend.* The object complement can be an adjective (or adjectival) or a noun (or nominal).

Interrogative: A structure-class word that introduces questions and certain nominal clauses: *where, when, who, what, why*, and *how*. For example, *Why is she leaving?*; *I wonder why she is leaving*.

Expletive: A word without semantic meaning used as a placeholder to fill the subject position at the beginning of an independent clause: *It is raining*; *There is a fly in my soup*.

Cluster III: Language

The following are terms that we need and like to use to talk about language. These terms are handy for thinking of grammar the way linguists do: as a dynamic social contract. The English language is a good sport, elastic and exuberant. In public and private discourse, we comfortably shift words from their original functions. Whereas traditional grammarians think of language in terms of "correct" or "incorrect," those of us who favor a more liberal view of the English language rejoice in its flexibility and ability to replenish itself through fresh usage and diction.

Rhetoric: The aspects of language use and organization that make it effective and persuasive for a particular audience and purpose; the study of those aspects.

Semantics: Meaning in language; the study of meaning in language.

Syntax: The structure and arrangement of words, phrases, and clauses in sentences; the study of this topic.

Form: The inherent features of grammatical units, as distinguished from their function. The forms of certain word classes are characterized by prefixes and suffixes. The forms of phrases are characterized by headwords and their objects, complements, or modifiers. The forms of clauses are characterized by subjects and predicates.

Form-class words: The four large classes of words that contribute the lexical content of the language: nouns, verbs, adjectives, and adverbs. They are also called *content words*. Each takes characteristic prefixes and suffixes that distinguish its form. New form-class words appear frequently, and they are sometimes called *open-class words* for this reason.

Function: The role of a word, phrase, or clause in a sentence. Consider the sentence *To wear a winter coat in the summer is bizarre behavior*. *To wear a winter coat in the summer* is an infinitive verb phrase that functions as the subject of the sentence. *Winter* in *winter coat* is a noun that functions adjectivally, modifying *coat*. *In the summer* is a prepositional phrase that functions as an adverbial modifier of *to wear*.

Structure-class words: The classes of words that show the grammatical or structural relationships between form-class words. The major structure classes are conjunctions, prepositions, auxiliaries, determiners, qualifiers, interrogatives, and expletives. New structure-class words appear rarely, and for this reason they are referred to as closed classes.

Coherence: The quality of being orderly, logical, and consistent.

Cohesion: The grammatical and semantic connections between sentences and paragraphs. Cohesive ties are furnished by pronouns that have antecedents in previous sentences, by adverbial connections, by known information, by repeated or related words, and by knowledge shared with the reader.

Parallelism: Two or more of the same grammatical structures that are coordinated—given equal weight—within a sentence, as in *He came early and left late; My words went in one ear and out the other*. The term also applies to repeated structures in separate sentences within a paragraph.

Referent: The referent is the thing that a word, phrase, or clause (or symbol) stands for, or names, within the text. The *antecedent*, then, is the word, phrase, or clause whose denotation is referred to by a pronoun.

Cluster IV: Structure of Words

English is a language that, unlike Latin, relies on word order rather than inflectional suffixes to signify grammatical function. Nevertheless, discussions about grammar need to include a few terms about units of meaning (morphemes) that attach to words.

Affix: A meaningful unit that is added to the beginning (prefix) or end (suffix) of a word to change its meaning or its function or its part of speech: (prefix) *un*helpful; (suffix) *unhelpful*.

    Prefix: A meaningful unit added to the beginning of a word to change its meaning (*il*legal) or its class (*en*able).

    Suffix: A meaningful unit added to the end of a word to change its class (*laugh—laughable*), its function (*eat—eating*), or its meaning (*dog—dogs*).

    Combining form: A combining form is a (usually Latin) root, part of a word that recombines to form related words.

Inflectional suffix: A suffix added to a noun (*-s* plural, *'s* possessive), verb (*-s*, *-ed*, *-ing*), or adjective and adverb (*-er* comparative, *-est* superlative) that alters its grammatical role or meaning: *Dog, dogs; walk, walked*.

Cluster V: Conjunctions

A great deal of grammar instruction involves teaching students how to punctuate sentence elements where conjunctions are used. As students become more sophisticated writers, they use more kinds of conjunctions.

Conjunction: A structure-class word that connects two or more words, phrases, or clauses.

Conjunctive adverb: A conjunction with an adverbial emphasis (*however, therefore, nevertheless, moreover,* etc.) that connects two clauses, as in *Chocolate is delicious; however, I try my best to stay away from it.*

Coordinating conjunction: A conjunction that connects two words, phrases, or clauses as equals: *and, but, or, nor, for, so,* and *yet.* For example, *Abraham and Jeff worked Tuesday.*

Correlative conjunction: A two-part conjunction: *either-or; neither-nor; both-and; not only- but also.* For example, *Neither the sofa nor that table looks right in this corner.*

Subordinating conjunction: A conjunction that introduces a subordinate clause. Among the most common, both simple and compound, are *after, although, as long as, because, before, if, since, so that, provided that, though, until, when, whenever,* and *while.*

Relative pronoun: The pronouns *who, whose, whom, that,* and *which,* used to introduce relative clauses: *The boy who lives here is named Jorge.*

Cluster VI: Clause Boundary Errors

Clause boundary errors—comma splices, run-on sentences, and fragments—are some of our most vexing problems in student writing.

Comma splice: Two independent clauses joined only by a comma, as in *Juanita went home, she has a doctor's appointment for her son.*

Run-on sentence: Two independent clauses with no punctuation between them, as in *Juanita went home she has a doctor's appointment for her son.*

Fragment: A group of words that, although punctuated as if it were a sentence, is not a complete sentence. Some fragments are dependent clauses: *She drove frantically to the store. Because she had run out of bread for tomorrow's lunches.* Others are phrases, without a subject and complete verb: *She went to get bread for tomorrow's lunches. Driving frantically to the store.* While most fragments are the result of punctuation or structural error, they can be used purposefully by experienced writers for stylistic reasons. For example: *We will accept absolutely no excuses. Except maybe one.* Here, the fragment has the humorous rhetorical effect of sounding like an afterthought.

Tag question: A two- or three-word question that verifies the truth of the statement that precedes it and to which it refers. If the statement is *You live in New Jersey*, the tag question would be *Don't you?* If the statement is *You are not from Wisconsin*, the tag question would be *Are you?* Tag questions can also demonstrate for students how much they "know" about pronouns and auxiliaries, etc.: *Joey and Fred have finished their homework, haven't they?* If you can add a tag question to a group of words, then that group of words is probably a complete sentence. Therefore, we can teach students to use the "tag question test" to test for sentence completeness.

Cluster VII: Agreement Conditions

Another cause of vexation is the subject-verb and pronoun-antecedent mismatch. The former transgressions arise most commonly when there are intervening words between the subject and verb. The latter generally come from the tendency to consider collective pronouns (*everybody*, *everyone*) plural rather than singular, and the tendency to match such collective pronouns with *their*, *they*, and *them*, as in *Everyone sat down when the teacher told them to*. Most progressive grammarians recognize that the language is moving toward acceptance of this widespread usage.

Subject-verb agreement: The matching of the number and person of the subject to the form of the verb. When the subject is third-person singular and the verb is in the present tense, the verb takes the *-s* inflection, as in *The dog barks all night*. He *bothers the neighbors*. With other subjects and in other tenses, verbs (with the exception of *be*) do not change to match the number or person of the subject: *I sleep; we sleep; he slept; they slept*. In the African American English dialect, "the *-s* ending is not required to show that a verb takes a third person singular subject in the present tense. Thus, in AAE, present-tense verbs are usually identical: *I walk, you walk, he walk, we walk, they walk*" (Redd and Webb 35).

Pronoun-antecedent agreement: The matching of the number (whether singular or plural) of the pronoun to the number of its antecedent: *The boys did their chores; Each girl did her best*.

Cluster VIII: Nominals

It is useful to think of a nominal—whether it be a single word (noun), noun phrase, or nominal clause—as a structure that can be replaced by *it* or *they*.

Nominal: A word, phrase, or clause that functions as a noun phrase does. Nominals do not necessarily contain nouns: *Traveling can be hard work; I'll accept whoever volunteers*. Nominals can perform seven functions: subject, subject complement, object of preposition, appositive, direct object, indirect object, object complement.

Noun: A form-class word that can usually be made plural or possessive, as in *boy/boys/boy's*. Nouns fill the headword slot in noun phrases (*my old Kentucky home*); they can also serve as adjectivals (*the home team*) and adverbials (*They went home*).

Noun phrase: The noun headword together with all of its modifiers. In the sentence *The gardener trimmed the pine tree with the broken branches, the gardener* is a noun phrase that functions as the sentence subject, and its headword is *gardener. The pine tree with the broken branches* is a noun phrase functioning as a direct object, and its headword is *tree. The broken branches* is a noun phrase that functions as the object of the preposition *with*, and its headword is *branches*.

Nominal clause: A clause that fills one of the seven nominal functions, often a *that* clause or an interrogative clause, as in *I know that she knows* (direct object); *Why they were late is none of my business* (subject).

Cluster IX: Pronouns

Most elementary students can parrot the traditional definition of a pronoun: "A pronoun is a word that takes the place of a noun." Problem is, that's not exactly true. While a pronoun certainly can take the place of a noun, more accurately, what a pronoun does is take the place of a *nominal*: a noun, noun phrase, or noun clause.

Pronoun: A word that substitutes for a nominal, as in *Sam tried to stop laughing, but he couldn't do it*. Types of pronouns include demonstrative pronouns (*this, these, that, those*), personal pronouns (*I, me, it, you*, etc.), indefinite pronouns (*every, everyone, many, any*, etc.), relative pronouns (*who, that, which*), and reflexive pronouns (*myself, yourself, himself*, etc.).

Case: A feature of nouns and certain pronouns (personal and relative pronouns) that is determined by the role the noun or pronoun fills in the sentence. Pronouns have three case distinctions: subjective (for example, *he, we, who*), possessive (*his, our, whose*), and objective (*him, us, whom*). Nouns have only one case inflection, the possessive (*John's, the cat's*).

Subjective case: **The role of a noun phrase or a pronoun when it functions as the subject of a clause. Personal pronouns have distinctive forms for subjective case:** *I, he, she, we, they*. **For example,** *She and Tom are happy*.

Objective case: **The role in a sentence of a noun phrase or pronoun when it functions as an object—direct object, indirect object, object complement, or object of a preposition. Personal pronouns and the relative pronoun** *who* **have special forms for the objective case:** *me, him, her, us*, **and** *them*, **as well as** *whom*. **For example,** *He gave him a stereo for his birthday; Hemingway's* For Whom the Bell Tolls *is a great novel*.

Possessive case: **The form of the noun (or pronoun) capable of signifying that it is owned by the noun (or pronoun) that follows it. We use the apostrophe *s* or the *s* apostrophe to signify the possessive case of nouns. Possessive case pronouns do not use apostrophe *s*. That no apostrophe *s* is used with possessive case pronouns is the reason for much confusion over the use of *its*:** *The cat chased <u>its</u> tail.*

Relative pronoun: The pronouns *who, whose, whom, that,* and *which,* used to introduce relative clauses: *The boy <u>who</u> lives here is named Jorge.*

Antecedent: The word or phrase, usually a noun phrase or other nominal, that a pronoun stands for: *Here is <u>your present</u>. I hope that you like <u>it</u>. <u>Traveling</u> can be hard work; in fact, <u>it</u> can be exhausting.*

Object of a preposition: All prepositional phrases end with a noun or pronoun or other nominal called the object of the preposition: *After <u>dinner</u> we are going to the movies. After <u>seeing the movie</u>, we will have dessert.*

Appositive: A structure that adds information by renaming another structure, as in *Ginger, <u>my dog</u>, is sweet but stubborn.* Or, *My daily exercise routine<u>, running around the track</u>, sometimes gets very boring.*

Headword: The main word of a phrase, the one that the others modify or complement. In the sentence *The boys in the parade waved to the crowd, boys* is the headword of the noun phrase *The boys in the parade; in* is the headword of the prepositional phrase *in the parade,* and *waved* is the headword of the verb phrase *waved to the crowd.*

Cluster X: Modifiers

In addition to the modifiers defined below, don't forget that a prepositional phrase is also a kind of modifier, one that can act adjectivally (when making the noun more specific) or adverbially (when answering the questions *where? when? how? to what extent?*): *The boys <u>from the band</u>; the clouds <u>in the distance</u>; my cousin <u>from Boston</u>.*

Modifier: A word, phrase, or clause that adds information about a noun or verb or the sentence as a whole: *The <u>blue</u> chair <u>that I bought at the auction</u> needs painting; The tomatoes grow <u>fast when the nights are warm</u>; <u>Unfortunately</u>, she lost her job.*

Adverb: A form-class word that generally modifies a verb, as in *I will be going <u>soon</u>.* Adverbs can also modify the sentence as a whole, as in *<u>Unfortunately</u>, I was out when you phoned.* Some adverbs can be compared (*more quickly*) or intensified (*very quickly*). Their position in the sentence is often flexible (*I will <u>soon</u> be going; <u>Soon</u> I will be going*).

Adverbial: Any structure (word, phrase, or clause) that functions as a modifier of a verb—that is, that fills the role of an adverb. In *We drove <u>to the airport</u> <u>to pick up Uncle Louis</u>, to the airport* is an adverbial prepositional phrase, and *to pick up Uncle Louis* is an adverbial infinitive phrase, both modifying the verb *drove*.

Particle: Any of various words accompanying the verb as part of a phrasal verb, such as *on* in *catch on* and *up* and *with* in *put up with*.

Cluster XI: Adjectives and Determiners

The traditional definition of an adjective is that it is a word that modifies a noun. Some teachers of traditional grammar define an adjective as a word that answers these questions: *Which one? What kind? How many?* When word groups, such as phrases or clauses, do the work of adjectives, we call such groups adjectivals.

Adjective: A form-class word that functions as a noun modifier. Adjectives can be made comparative and superlative (*tall, taller, tallest*) and can be qualified or intensified (*very tall*).

Adjectival: Any structure (word, phrase, or clause) that fills the role of an adjective—that is, that functions as an adjective normally does, modifying a noun: *The house on the corner is new.* In this sentence, *on the corner* is an adjectival prepositional phrase; *on the corner* tells us *which one*.

Determiner: A structure-class word that marks or signals a noun, appearing as the first word in a noun phrase, before the noun and before any modifiers in the phrase. Determiners include the articles *a, an,* and *the* and those words that can be used in their place: demonstrative pronouns, indefinite pronouns, numbers, possessive pronouns, and possessive nouns. For example, *The telephone is a wonderful invention; This darned telephone doesn't work; Some cell phones are expensive; We have three blue, cordless telephones; You're using my cell phone; Conchita's phone doesn't work anymore.*

Article: The determiners *a* and *an* (the indefinite articles) and *the* (the definite article): *A View to a Kill; The Man with the Golden Gun.*

Qualifier: A structure-class word that qualifies or intensifies adjectives and adverbs, as in *We worked very hard; Joan was slightly annoyed; It's much colder today.*

Whole sentence modifier: A word, phrase, or clause that modifies the sentence as a whole rather than a particular structure within it. It is sometimes called a free modifier: *Ironically, the other team won; In an ironic turn of events, the other team won.*

Dangling participle: A participial phrase at the beginning or end of a sentence in which the subject of the sentence is not the subject of the participle. In other words, a dangling participle is a verb without a subject, as in **Walking through the woods, the moon shone brightly.*

Nonrestrictive modifier: A modifier—a word, phrase, or clause—in the noun phrase that comments on the noun but is not necessary for defining or identifying it. It is set off with commas: *The Finance Committee, which met last week, is still working on the budget.*

Restrictive modifier: A modifier—a word, phrase, or clause—in the noun phrase that restricts and identifies the referent of the noun. It is not set off by commas: *Homer's epic poem <u>The Odyssey</u> is a great book to teach; The chair <u>that you just sat on</u> is broken.*

Cluster XII: Verbs

The following terms allow us to speak about what verbs can do. Verbs can be divided into two categories in various ways: Is the verb finite or nonfinite? Action or linking? If action, is it transitive or intransitive? Is the verb regular or irregular? In the active or the passive voice?

Verb: A form-class word that names an action, process, or state; that can always take both *-s* and *-ing* endings; and that can be signaled by auxiliary verbs: *It <u>goes</u>; She is <u>going</u>; We should <u>go</u>.*

Base form of the verb: The uninflected form of the verb, as it appears in the frame "To_____is difficult." The base form appears in the infinitive (*To <u>be</u> or not to <u>be</u>*), in the present tense for all persons except third-person singular (*I <u>walk</u>, you <u>walk</u>, we <u>walk</u>, they <u>walk</u>*), and in other verb phrases following modal auxiliaries (*He must <u>walk</u>; They will <u>walk</u>*).

> **Base form**
> *-ing* form (present participle; this is also used with an auxiliary)
> *-s* form (present tense, used in third-person singular)
> *-ed* form (past)
> *-en* form (past participle, used with an auxiliary)

Finite: Specific, or finite, as to tense. Verbs in the present tense or past tense are finite verbs: *He <u>filled</u> the tub.* Phrases with such verbs are finite verb phrases. In most finite verb phrases, the first verb is the only finite verb: *He <u>had</u> filled the tub.* (*Filled* in this sentence is a past participle.) Modals, which begin many verb phrases, are not as clear as to their finiteness. They don't take endings that indicate the past or present tense, but some of them suggest past, present, or future time as well as possibility or probability. For example, *She can go* can refer to the present or the future but not the past.

Nonfinite: Not definite as to tense. The nonfinite verbs are infinitives, participles, and gerunds. Nonfinite verbs appear in the main verb phrase, where they are preceded by a finite verb (one with tense), as in *Melissa is <u>running</u> in the race* (present participle). They also appear in other phrases where they function nominally, adjectivally, or adverbially; such phrases are nonfinite verb phrases: *Yuri loves <u>to sing</u>* (infinitive as direct object); *The <u>snoring</u> man is next door* (present participle as modifier of *man*); *She likes <u>riding</u> roller coasters* (gerund as direct object).

Action verb: A verb that expresses action (something that can be done).

> **Transitive verb:** A verb that requires a direct object as its complement to be complete, as in *He drove the car*. Many verbs can be either transitive or intransitive: *Charles drove.* Most transitive verbs can be made passive: *The car was driven by Charles*.

> **Intransitive verb:** A verb that has no complement, although it may take an adverbial modifier: *Denzel's parents arrived at the airport*.

Linking verb: A verb that links the complement to the sentence subject, as in *The chicken is tasty; The salad looks delicious; The chef just became my husband*.

Auxiliary (helping) verb: A structure-class word used with verbs. Auxiliary verbs include *have, be,* and *do* when they are used in phrases with other verbs, as well as such modals as *will* and *must*: *Miguel will have left by tomorrow. Do you need to see him?*

Modal: An auxiliary verb that opens a main verb string and that conveys the probability, possibility, obligation, or other mood of the main verb. The principal modals are *can, could, will, would, shall, should, may, might,* and *must*: e.g., *He should be here. He said he would be. He must be sick.* Other kinds of modals include *need* and *dare,* as in *You need not have said that* and *I don't dare say it.* Modal phrases include *have to,* as in *Anita has to leave*.

"Do" support: We use the word *do* to form a question (*Do you like ice cream?*), to emphasize (*I told you that I do like ice cream*), to form a tag question when there is no auxiliary (*I spent all my money on ice cream, didn't I?*), and to substitute for a verb phrase that has been previously mentioned (*Do you take this woman to be your lawfully wedded wife? I do.*).

Present tense: The base form (*eat*) along with the -s form (*eats*) that is used with a third-person singular subject. The present tense denotes a present point in time (*I like your new hairdo*), a habitual action (*My parents live in Arizona*), or the "timeless" present (*The earth revolves around the sun*).

Progressive: A verb construction consisting of the auxiliary *be* and the present participle, expressing a present or past ongoing activity or a temporary state, as in *Jamal is eating; Molly was being silly*.

Participle: The verb forms that appear in verb phrases after the auxiliary verbs *to be,* as in *I was eating* (present participle), and *to have,* as in *I have eaten* (past participle). *Participle is* also the term used to refer to the present or past participle in its role as an adjectival, as a modifier in the noun phrase: *The band members, wearing their snazzy new uniforms, proudly marched onto the field*.

Present participle: The *-ing* form of the verb used with the auxiliary *be*: *We are going; They should be leaving soon*. This *-ing* form of the verb is also used as an adjectival modifier as well as a main verb: *Leaving the park, she was feeling the excitement of the city*. The word *present* in the label for this verb form does not denote present time, and in fact the present participle is not definite as to time: *He is leaving; He was leaving*.

Past participle: The form of the verb used with the auxiliary *have*: *We have for-gotten something*; *We have walked two miles*. The past participle can stand on its own, without *have*, when used as a passive participle (adjectival): *For-gotten by his friends, he lived alone*. The past participle is also used with a form of *to be* in the passive voice, as in *The car was fixed by the mechanic*. Even though the past participles that end in *-ed* have the same form as the past tense of regular verbs, the word *past* in the name of this verb form does not denote past time: *We have walked* (past participle); *We walked* (past tense); *The dog is walked by the girl next door* (present tense, passive voice).

Verbal: Another term given to nonfinite verbs—participles, gerunds, and in-finitives—when their function is other than that of main verb: as adjectivals, adverbials, or nominals.

Infinitive: The base form of the verb often preceded by *to*: *To die, to sleep;* / *To sleep: perchance to dream; ay, there's the rub.*

Infinitive phrase: The infinitive together with all of its complements and modifiers. Infinitive phrases function as adverbials, adjectivals, and nominals: *Rajesh wants to watch his favorite TV show* (infinitive phrase as direct object).

Gerund: An *-ing* verb functioning as a nominal—that is, as a noun functions: *I enjoy reading*; *Playing the piano is relaxing*.

Gerund Phrase: A gerund together with all of its complements and modifi-ers, as in *Playing the piano is relaxing*.

Voice: When we speak of the "voice" of a verb, we are speaking of whether it is active or passive voice:

Active voice: A feature of sentences in which the subject performs the ac-tion of the verb and the direct object is the goal or the recipient: *The me-chanic fixed the car*.

Passive voice: A feature of sentences in which the object or goal of the ac-tion functions as the sentence subject, and the main verb phrase includes the verb *to be* and the past participle, as in *The car was fixed by the mechanic*.

Phrasal verb: A verb consisting of a verb plus a particle or particles: *look up* the statistics, *give in to* the pressure, *put up* with the noise, *find out* the truth, *make up* a lie, *turn in* at midnight, *come by* a fortune, *go in* for horse racing, and many other everyday verbs.

Main verb string: The part of the sentence consisting of the main verb and any auxiliary verbs that precede it: *Tyrone tried hard*; *Sheila should have been trying harder*.

Main verb: The verb that fills the last position in the main verb string, or the only position if there are no auxiliary verbs. Sometimes called the lexical verb, it carries the specific meaning about actions, events, or states of be-ing, as in *Raheem has been writing a short story. He told me about it.*

Regular verb: A verb that forms the past tense and past participle by the addition of *-ed* (or, in a few cases, *-d* or *-t*) to the base form: *Yesterday, he <u>walked</u> to school; Maria has <u>walked</u> all the way.*

Irregular verb: A verb that does not form its past tense and past participle by adding *-ed, -d,* or *-t,* as regular verbs do: *Sing, sang, sung; go, went, gone.*

References

Benjamin, Amy. *Writing Put to the Test: Teaching for the High Stakes Essay.* Larchmont, NY: Eye on Education, 2006.

Caine, Renate Nummela, Geoffrey Caine, Carol Lynn McClintic, and Karl J. Klimek. *12 Brand/Mind Learning Principles in Action: The Fieldbook for Making Connections, Teaching, and the Human Brain.* Thousand Oaks, CA: Corwin, 2004.

Capote, Truman. *In Cold Blood: A True Account of a Multiple Murder and Its Consequences.* New York: Random House, 1965.

Crystal, David. *The Cambridge Encyclopedia of the English Language.* Cambridge, UK: Cambridge UP, 2004.

Dykstra, Pamela. *Rhythms of Writing.* Boston: Houghton Mifflin, 2000.

Fries, Charles Carpenter. *The Structure of English: An Introduction to the Construction of English Sentences.* New York: Harcourt, Brace & World, 1952.

Gere, Anne Ruggles, Leila Christenbury, and Kelly Sassi. *Writing on Demand: Best Practices and Strategies for Success.* Portsmouth, NH: Heinemann, 2005.

Hairston, Maxine. "Not All Errors Are Created Equal: Nonacademic Readers in the Professions Respond to Lapses in Usage." *College English* 43 (1981): 794–806.

Hancock, Craig. *Meaning-Centered Grammar: An Introductory Text.* Oakville, CT: Equinox, 2005.

Haussamen, Brock. *Revising the Rules: Traditional Grammar and Modern Linguistics.* 2nd ed. Dubuque, IA: Kendall/Hunt, 1997.

Haussamen, Brock, with Amy Benjamin, Martha Kolln, Rebecca Wheeler, and ATEG. *Grammar Alive! A Guide for Teachers.* Urbana, IL: NCTE, 2003.

Hawthorne, Nathaniel. *The Scarlet Letter.* 1850. Cutchogue, NY: Buccaneer Books, 1997.

Jensen, Eric. *Teaching with the Brain in Mind.* Alexandria, VA: ASCD, 1998.

Joseph, Sister Miriam. *The Trivium: The Liberal Arts of Logic, Grammar, and Rhetoric: Understanding the Nature and Function of Language.* 1948. Ed. Marguerite McGlinn. Philadelphia: Paul Dry Books, 2002.

Kolln, Martha. *Rhetorical Grammar: Grammatical Choices, Rhetorical Effects.* 5th ed. New York: Pearson Education, 2007.

Mulroy, David. *The War against Grammar.* Portsmouth, NH: Boynton/Cook, 2003.

National Council of Teachers of English. Resolution "On the Students' Right to Their Own Language." 1974. 24 Oct. 2006 <http://www.ncte.org/about/over/positions/category/lang/107502.htm?source=gs>.

Noguchi, Rei R. *Grammar and the Teaching of Writing: Limits and Possibilities.* Urbana, IL: NCTE, 1991.

Perry, Theresa, and Lisa Delpit, eds. *The Real Ebonics Debate: Power, Language, and the Education of African-American Children.* Boston: Beacon, 1998.

Pugh, Sharon L., Jean Wolph Hicks, and Marcia Davis. *Metaphorical Ways of Knowing: The Imaginative Nature of Thought and Expression.* Urbana, IL: NCTE, 1997.

Pugh, Sharon L., Jean Wolph Hicks, Marcia Davis, and Tonya Venstra. *Bridging: A Teacher's Guide to Metaphorical Thinking.* Urbana, IL: NCTE, 1992.

Ray, Katie Wood. *Wondrous Words: Writers and Writing in the Elementary Classroom.* Urbana, IL: NCTE, 1999.

Redd, Teresa M., and Karen Schuster Webb. *A Teacher's Introduction to African American English: What a Writing Teacher Should Know.* Urbana, IL: NCTE, 2005.

Remarque, Erich Maria. *All Quiet on the Western Front.* 1929. New York: Ballantine, 1982.

Rowling, J. K. *Harry Potter and the Half-Blood Prince.* New York: Arthur A. Levine, 2005.

Rickford, John. "The Oakland Ebonics Decision: Commendable Attack on the Problem." *The San Jose Mercury News* 26 Dec. 1996.

Strunk, William, and E. B. White. *The Elements of Style.* New York: Macmillan, 1959.

Sweetland, Julie. "The Words We Choose to Use Lesson Plan." *Sociolinguistic Sensitivity in Language Arts Instruction: A Literature and Writing Curriculum for the Intermediate Grades, Teachers' Manual and Materials.* Unpublished ms, Dept. of Linguistics, Stanford U.

Taylor, Hanni. *Standard English, Black English, and Bidialectalism: A Controversy.* New York: Peter Lang, 1989.

Wheeler, Rebecca S., and Rachel Swords. "Codeswitching: Tools of Language and Culture Transform the Dialectally Diverse Classroom." *Language Arts* 81.6 (2004): 470–80.

White, E. B. *Charlotte's Web.* 1952. New York: HarperCollins, 1980.

Wiggins, Grant, and McTighe, Jay. *Understanding by Design Handbook.* Alexandria, VA: ASCD, 1999.

Index

Authors

Amy Benjamin has received awards for excellence in teaching from the New York State English Council, Tufts University, and Union College. She currently serves as president of NCTE's Assembly for the Teaching of English Grammar and is a coauthor of NCTE's *Grammar Alive! A Guide for Teachers*. Benjamin is an educational consultant for NCTE's Professional Development Consulting Network. She lives with her husband Howard in the beautiful Hudson Valley in New York. Her professional website is www.amybenjamin.com.

Tom Oliva is an English teacher and avid music enthusiast. He teaches at Hendrick Hudson High School, where he also advises the Literary Magazine and Film Club. In his spare time, he enjoys the outdoors, writing poetry, and amateur musical endeavors. Oliva grew up in southern New Jersey but now resides in the quaint Hudson Valley hamlet of Fort Montgomery with his wife Christine and their son Jackson Phoenix.

This book was typeset in Palatino and Helvetica by Electronic Imaging.
Typefaces used on the cover include Frutiger and Century Schoolbook.
The book was printed on 50-lb. White Williamsburg Offset paper
by Versa Press, Inc.